THE GRAMMAR PLAN BOOK

THE GRAMMAR PLAN BOOK

A Guide to Smart Teaching

CONSTANCE WEAVER

HEINEMANN
Portsmouth, NH

Heinemann

A division of Reed Elsevier Inc.

361 Hanover Street

Portsmouth, NH 03801–3912

www.heinemann.com

Offices and agents throughout the world

The author and publisher wish to thank those who have generously given permission to reprint borrowed material:

Excerpts from *Mechanically Inclined: Building Grammar, Usage, and Style into Writer's Workshop* by Jeff Anderson. Copyright © 2005, with permission of Stenhouse Publishers.

Figure 2–7: "Twenty Errors Most Commonly Marked by College Teachers" list from *The St. Martin's Handbook 5th edition* by Andrea Lunsford. Copyright © 2003 by Bedford/St. Martin's. Reproduced by permission of Bedford/St. Martin's.

Excerpts from *Circle of Magic: Sandry's Book* by Tamora Pierce. Copyright © 1997 by Tamora Pierce. Reprinted by permission of Scholastic Inc.

Figure D–1: "Code-Switching Shopping List" chart from *Code-Switching: Teaching Standard English in Urban Classrooms* by Rebecca Wheeler and Rachel Swords. Copyright © 2006 by the National Council of Teachers of English. Reprinted with permission.

Library of Congress Cataloging-in-Publication Data
Weaver, Constance.
  The grammar plan book : a guide to smart teaching / Constance Weaver.
      p.   cm.
  Includes bibliographical references and index.
  ISBN-13: 978-0-325-01043-4 (acid-free paper)
  ISBN-10: 0-325-01043-9
  1. English language—Rhetoric—Study and teaching.   2. English
language—Grammar—Study and teaching.   I. Title.
  PE1404.W42 2006
  428.2071—dc22   2006021831

Editor: Lisa Luedeke
Production management: Sarah Weaver
Production coordination: Abigail M. Heim
Typesetter: Technologies 'N Typography
Interior and cover design: Catherine Hawkes, Cat & Mouse
Manufacturing: Jamie Carter

Printed in the United States of America on acid-free paper

10 09 08 07 06 ML 1 2 3 4 5

For Samantha Arwen and Caiden Timothy

Contents

PART TWO The Grammar Planner

Grammar to Expand and Enrich Writing: Putting First Things First 75

The Sentence: Structure, Organization, Punctuation—and More 95

Grammatical Considerations in Choosing the Right Words 114

D

More on Style, Rhetoric, and Conventions   128

As Katherine Baer (a secondary English resource teacher for the Howard County Public School System in Ellicott City, Maryland) and I began to correspond about integrating literature and grammar with writing instruction, she made this apt characterization in an email dated May 26, 2005: "Many experienced teachers need to 'unlearn' the tactic of drilling parts of speech, many mid-career teachers usually incorporate only small doses of language instruction because of their uncertainties about syntax, and many of our young teachers know precious little about grammar."

Precisely, I thought.

Teachers who have long taught traditional grammar need to be persuaded, perhaps through examples, that teaching less grammar but teaching it throughout the writing process can do much more for students' writing than teaching grammar in isolation. Midcareer teachers have likely heard the slogan "teach grammar in the context of writing," but they may be concerned about the adequacy of their own grammar knowledge or at least uncertain how, exactly, to start teaching grammatical options and skills while helping students draft, revise, and edit. And many younger teachers have little or no conscious knowledge of grammar to draw on as they attempt to help students enrich and enhance their writing.

This book is designed for all three audiences. Part 1 includes many examples of how less grammar can do more for students' writing when taught throughout the writing process and over time. The section concludes with a chapter on making smart decisions about what editing skills to teach and—with regard to test preparation—includes an informal examination and weighting of what kinds of grammar items typically are included on one such test, the ACT. Part 2, the Grammar Planner, is both a handbook of grammatical concepts and a planning document where teachers can indicate what aspects of grammar they intend to teach and when. It is followed by a brief planning checklist (a "scope" and potential sequence) that teachers—working individually or together—can use to record their decisions about teaching grammar.

Part 2 is organized according to what needs to be taught first in the writing process—expanding and enriching content—and afterward attending to revision and editing. This Grammar Planner includes most of the grammatical concepts that middle school and secondary teachers need to know as teachers of writing, along with advice for distinguishing between what constitutes good writing and what is required for scoring high on some standardized tests of revision and editing skills—like the ACT and the SAT. I argue that writing instruction should not be limited by such tests, which include items on "rules that do not rule" (Schuster, 2003); see Section D.

Those who have contributed to this work are many:

- My colleague Jonathan Bush, who has not only offered valuable insights but inspired the book's subtitle and the focus of Chapter 1.
- My own college students and younger students from grade four upward.
- Sixth-grade teacher Jeff Anderson, from Rayburn Middle School in San Antonio, who wrote a section on editing.
- Two teachers from the Hudsonville, Michigan, Public Schools: Rebecca Schipper, who reported on her successes with ninth graders, and Jeff Henderson, who worked with me to teach participial phrases to his sixth graders. (Special thanks also to their language arts consultant, Cheryl-Marie Gunnett.)
- Sarah Cauldwell, Betty Roberts, and Julie Kast, from the Greenwich Country Day School in Greenwich, Connecticut. Their contributions also enabled me to demonstrate what it can look like to teach grammar in the context of writing.

I especially want also to thank the wonderful people at Heinemann. Lisa Luedeke, my editor, never failed to encourage me through her positive responses to my work; she is an absolute gem. Alan Huisman is, quite simply, the best developmental editor I have ever had: He has tightened my writing to a degree I never would have believed possible. Gratitude goes also to Abby Heim, Sarah Weaver, and Cathy Hawkes, the best production coordinator, production manager, and designer I have ever had.

Finally, I wish once again to acknowledge the undying influence of my first professional mentor, Owen Thomas, who not only inspired me but taught me to believe in myself. And I am especially grateful to those who currently love and support me, particularly Rolland Batdorff and my son and daughter-in-law, John and Chris. It is to their children, my grandchildren, that this book is dedicated.

Smart Teachers in Action

A Third Way

All too often, my colleague Jonathan Bush writes, we see classrooms where grammar is "covered." Parallelism? "Oh, yes. We covered that." Fragments and comma splices? "We did those in October." Subject-verb agreement? Joining clauses and sentences? "Those were part of last year's curriculum. My students should already know them."

If such teacher responses do not sound familiar, then perhaps you are hearing, or thinking, "Grammar? We're not supposed to teach that." Or, "Students already know grammar." Or, "I can write just fine without knowing grammar. Why should I teach it to my students?"

On the one hand, traditional methods of teaching grammar from A to Z, from September through December—or June—have not worked very well to improve students' writing. In fact, as we shall see in Chapter 1, teaching grammar as a method of teaching writing has had a negative effect on students' writing, perhaps because it has often replaced the genuine teaching of writing. But of course the opposite extreme has not been maximally effective, either. While students' abilities and potential to use the language more effectively don't necessarily shrivel up and die when neglected, neither do they fully bloom.

Is there a third alternative, a middle way? Of course—and not just one. Here are two key principles underlying the smart teaching of grammar as described in *this* book:

In teaching grammar for writing, less is more.

> —Rei Noguchi, *Grammar and the Teaching of Writing: Limits and Possibilities*, 1991

Teach an inch wide and a mile deep.

> —Theresa Reagan-Donk, Coordinator of Instruction for the Hudsonville, Michigan, public schools

The teacher narratives in Part 1 exemplify these principles. You are invited to join those of us who are experiencing close encounters of the third grammatical kind with our students—and loving it!

Grammar to Enrich and Enhance Writing

A Smart Perspective

What's the weather report? "Cloudy with a chance of meatballs," as in Judi Barrett's picture book by the same title? Hardly. How about "Sunny, with a chance of little yellow grammar modules falling from the sky?" No, not that either.

The major problem with those little grammar modules—yellow or not—is this: They present grammar in isolation, which is not the most productive or efficient way to get students to use grammar more effectively in their writing. While hardly any experimental research has directly addressed this question, the predominant conclusion from a century of research shows that teaching grammar in isolation, as a school subject, has little or no effect on most students' writing.

Again and again, researchers have summarized the research and come to essentially the same conclusion about the ineffectiveness, for writing, of teaching grammar in isolation. The latest of these studies was conducted at the University of York, in England, and published in 2004. The researchers conclude:

> In terms of practice, the main implication of our findings is that there is no high quality evidence that the teaching of grammar, whether traditional or generative/transformational, is worth the time if the aim is the improvement of the quality and/or accuracy of written composition. (Andrews et al., 2004b, p. 4)

Let me emphasize: Teaching grammar in isolation does not do much to enrich the quality of students' writing, nor does it do much to enhance its accuracy. In other words, isolated teaching of grammatical concepts associated with "standard" English does not make much of a difference in the forms students use when they write. Teachers need to make the connection explicit as they guide students in editing.

Hardly any experimental research has been done on the effects *on students' writing* of teaching grammar in isolation compared with teaching it in the context of writing. Perhaps the only substantial study is one conducted over several months in six schools, grades four through six. As reported by DiStefano and Killion (1984), the aim of the study was to see whether students would apply writing conventions better if these were taught in conjunction with students' writing instead of in isolation. At the end of the study, the only significant differences favored the classes

What is "grammar," anyway?

Fundamentally, the grammar of a language is its *structure*. It's the elements of the language and the structural "rules" for combining them—whether or not anybody understands those rules consciously. The term *grammar* is also used for *descriptions* of its structure—whether reasonably accurate or not. The best known but least helpful descriptions are those of traditional school grammar, which have persisted with little change for literally hundreds of years. When people talk about "teaching grammar," they commonly mean teaching traditional grammar, often in isolation from its practical uses.

that were taught grammatical conventions in the context of their use in writing.

Unfortunately, teachers are currently under increased pressure to prepare students for standardized tests of grammar. Politicians and the public don't know the research; they only know what they want: better writing that reflects the conventions of mainstream edited American English, or "standard" English as it's popularly called. Smart teachers, knowing that extensive isolated grammar instruction isn't very effective even for taking tests (McQuade, 1980), will teach grammar intertwined with writing, and, if necessary, separately help students prepare for such tests by teaching additional skills in the context of practice tests (keeping in mind that the better students can often teach themselves, using a practice-test book). This is certainly the most efficient use of instructional time and probably the most effective as well, with skills taught in the context of their use.

And indeed, after reiterating their conclusion that there is "no high quality evidence" that teaching any kind of grammar in isolation "is effective with regard to writing development," the authors of the York study advise:

> Having established that much, we can now go on to research what is effective, and to ask clearer and more pertinent questions about what works in the development of young people's literacy. (p. 5)

Meanwhile, what is the smart teacher to do?

What do smart teachers do about teaching grammar?

An obvious first question is, "What do you mean by a smart teacher?" In my opinion, smart teachers are those who, from research and experience,

- know kids and the different ways they learn best,
- know their subject, and
- know "best practice"—specifically, the best practices for accomplishing their instructional goals.

Smart teachers, in other words, operate from solid knowledge.

But I'd like to suggest that, at their best, smart teachers are also

- risk-takers and experimenters,
- innovators, and
- integrators within and across subject areas.

This means that smart teachers heed the research on teaching grammar in isolation. If their primary purpose for teaching grammar is to strengthen student writing, they do the best they can—under current political and administrative circumstances—to move away from teaching grammar in

1: Grammar to Enrich and Enhance Writing

isolation and experiment instead with ways of teaching less grammar but teaching it more effectively for writing—often by drawing on literary and other published texts for examples and by incorporating selected aspects of grammar into the teaching of writing. Some smart teachers and language arts consultants are even affecting how grammar is taught in their schools—and in their states!

Teaching certain kinds of grammatical constructions to enrich writing can strengthen students' writing by

- encouraging the addition of details (ideas) to make the writing more interesting;
- clarifying the relationships between and among ideas and enhancing organizational flow;
- helping create a particular style or voice; and
- promoting variety, fluency, and rhythm within sentences and paragraphs.

By first attending to such issues, we can help students produce pieces of writing that are worthy of being edited, proofread, and shared with an audience beyond just the teacher or just the teacher and classmates. In other words, as we help students edit their writing, we can also teach the grammar needed for understanding and applying the key conventions of grammar, usage (including word choices), punctuation, and spelling (the internal grammar of words) that are appropriate to purpose and audience.

In the forthcoming *Grammar to Enrich and Enhance Writing*, attention to details, style/voice, and sentence fluency are generally considered to be part of *grammar to **enrich** writing*, while reserving the phrase *grammar to **enhance** writing* for attention to editing conventions. In this book I follow the same practice.

Attention to the various aspects of grammar and related skills can strengthen—to a greater or lesser degree—all six of the "6 traits of writing" that are commonly taught and addressed:

- Ideas
- Organization
- Voice
- Word choice
- Sentence fluency
- Conventions

See, for example, Ruth Culham's *6 + 1 Traits of Writing* (2003) and Vicki Spandel's *Creative Writers Through 6-Trait Assessment and Instruction* (2005). Whether phrased the same or not, whether separate or combined, the topics in many of the current rubrics for assessing writing—in state writing assessments and in standardized tests, as well as in local classrooms—are typically similar, and most can be addressed by selective attention to grammar during the process of writing.

Whether phrased the same or not, whether separate or combined, the topics in many of the current rubrics for assessing writing . . . are typically similar, and most can be addressed by selective attention to grammar during the process of writing.

Increasingly, there are resources to help smart teachers with this challenge of teaching less grammar but teaching it more effectively for writing. See the recommendations at the end of this chapter.

Sentence combining: A first step in teaching grammar innovatively?

Various studies, based on the work of Francis Christensen (1967) and researchers John Mellon (1969) and Frank O'Hare (1973), have been conducted on the effects of sentence combining, mostly with positive results. Sentence combining is just what it sounds like: combining simple sentences to create sentences that are richer in detail and usually more sophisticated in structure. For example, I could write the following relatively simple sentences: *I stood where the waves lapped the shore of Lake Michigan. I gazed longingly across the golden path that beckoned me beyond the horizon. The path was created by the setting sun.* Or I could combine these sentences and write: *I stood where the waves lapped the shore of Lake Michigan, gazing longingly across the golden path created by the setting sun, which beckoned me beyond the horizon.*

Most of the research has focused on sentence combining done apart from writing. Such activities typically involve combining sets of simple sentences into a single sentence, imitating literary sentences, and expanding sentences with the addition of modifiers that students create themselves.

This approach is exemplified in a recent book by Don and Jenny Killgallon: *Grammar for Middle School: A Sentence-Composing Approach* (2006) provides literary models for imitation in sentence combining. For students at the middle school or secondary level, William Strong's *Sentence Combining: A Composing Book* (3d ed., 1994) has been a favorite since its initial publication in 1973. Strong's *Writer's Toolbox: A Sentence-Combining Workshop* (1996) provides activities for integrating sentence combining into different phases of the writing process, particularly in a workshop approach. Some of the activities invite students to recombine simple sentences derived from "well-crafted sentences by famous people" (p. 21). The Killgallons' book introduces but does not emphasize grammatical terminology, and Strong's *Sentence Combining* does not even use grammatical terminology: The books just help writers get the hang of producing more sophisticated sentences. Though it introduces grammatical terms, Strong's *Writer's Toolbox* does not emphasize terminology, either.

Sentence combining is the only kind of "grammar" teaching that has consistently been found helpful in enriching students' writing—or at least their writing of individual sentences. Actually, though, it is a technique not for teaching grammar but for teaching ways of making sentences more sophisticated and effective.

Sentence combining is often part of the lesson sequence illustrated in this book and in *Grammar to Enrich and Enhance Writing*. The big difference is that the Killgallon and Strong sentence-combining books could provide an entire course of study. My books recommend sentence combining and imitating before or while students draft their own pieces of writing and within the context of revising their own writing.

Though helping students imitate good model sentences and combine their own sentences may be most effective, smart teachers may find it easiest to begin with sentence combining as a technique for writing sentences that will contain richer ideas, contribute to sentence sophistication and fluency, and potentially contribute to voice as well. In any case, sentence-combining books can help teachers grasp how to lead students in imitating, combining, and expanding sentences, and the material from such books can be helpful for creating minilessons derived from the literature teachers use in their own classrooms and from students' own writing. Such books can serve as training wheels for the smart teacher.

Harry Noden's *Image Grammar Activities Book* (forthcoming) can take smart teachers a step farther.

Research on sentence combining

The York researchers did a separate study on the effect of sentence combining activities on the "syntactic maturity" of students' sentences. In seventeen of the eighteen studies that met their criteria for in-depth analysis, sentence combining did have positive effects. Of course the effects diminished over time, but the few studies that investigated whether the effects were maintained suggested at least some long-term carryover to students' writing (Andrews et al., 2004a, pp. 47–48). Few studies have investigated the effect of sentence combining on overall (holistic) writing quality, but two of the better-quality studies did find that students' compositions were rated higher after sentence combining (O'Hare, 1973; Combs, 1976, 1977).

On the other hand, in one study an entire semester of sentence-combining practice had effects not much different from those of a week spent intensively helping college students combine, expand, and revise the sentences in their own writing, in connection with teacher advice to use longer, more complex sentences in their writing (Smith & Hull, 1985). In short, the approach demonstrated in this book and in *Grammar to Enrich and Enhance Writing* may be not only sufficient but much more time effective in the long run. One study does indicate that combining someone else's sentences is not necessarily as effective as imitating model sentences, at least in certain instances (Williams, 1986), and another study suggests that extensive reading and writing may be just as helpful as sentence combining, if not moreso (Hartwell & LoPresti, 1985). This suggests but does not "prove" that having students create their own sentences may be more effective than having them use sentence-combining books.

Principles to guide the smart teaching of grammar for writing

Drawn from research and experience, the following observations about the teaching of grammar may be taken as principles to guide the smart teaching of grammar for improving writing. Because of the intended brevity of this book, the principles are not discussed in much detail but simply offered for your consideration.

Ten observations and principles drawn from research, observation, and experience

1. Grammar taught in isolation from writing does not produce significant improvements in writing (with the exception of sentence combining, which is a technique for writing sentences, not teaching grammar). It is both more motivating and more practical to teach selected aspects of grammar in conjunction with the writing process by

providing examples of good writing and minilessons, and by conferencing with students.

2. It is better to teach a few things repeatedly and well than a lot of grammatical terms that have little or no practical relevance to writing. Equally important: We must realize that by no means all the constructions that students use in their writing need to be taught. More and more students spontaneously demonstrate command of grammatical options when they have rich opportunities to read and discuss the craft of good literature.

3. It is not realistic to expect students to master something that is taught just once. Many repetitions may be necessary, in different meaningful contexts and over several school months and years.

4. Whenever possible, students who have already mastered a construction or skill should be taught something they have not yet mastered rather than what other classmates still need to learn. Grammatical constructions, revision techniques, and editing skills should be taught as students are developmentally ready for them and have practical need for them, not according to an arbitrary scope-and-sequence chart.

5. Grammatical constructions and skills that are important for writing should be taught in conjunction with writing and reinforced over several grade levels, allowing for more and more students to achieve at least a reasonable level of competence in their use.

6. In many schools and classrooms, grammatical constructions and skills can be first taught at earlier grade levels than specified in the average scope-and-sequence chart. Early teaching to students who appear ready allows them to progress faster and offers the possibility of earlier "mastery," as well as greater progress toward mastery over time by more students.

7. Repeatedly teaching editing skills in conjunction with the editing process is more effective in producing independent application than teaching the skills in isolation (a variation of item 1). Marking up student papers with corrections is not a productive way of teaching editing skills.

8. English language learners (those learning English as a second or subsequent language) should be taught ways of making their sentences more interesting, not just ways of making their sentences more correct. The same is true for other students who may need explicit help in using "standard" English forms when they edit and write.

9. When we teach the use of new kinds of grammatical constructions in writing, many students may at first make new kinds of errors. Their risk taking needs to be honored and celebrated for them to continue to progress. And then we need to reteach the concept as many times as necessary.

10. We teachers need to serve as role models, sharing our own drafts and revision/editing strategies as well as final pieces. Teacher-written models for imitation are also a strong motivator.

You might reread these principles, deciding which are the most important for guiding your own teaching of grammar in smarter and smarter ways.

How this book can help you

First, let me tell you what this book does *not* do:

1. It does not offer a complete grammar of the English language or even as complete a grammar as is typically found in high school or college handbooks. This brevity reflects the principle that less is more.
2. It does not describe all the conventions that teachers of the elementary and intermediate grades might want to teach, particularly in terms of capitalization, contractions, abbreviations, and such. (These aspects of "mechanics" are often considered part of "grammar," though strictly speaking they are not.)
3. It does not treat in detail a specific methodology for teaching the conventions of edited American English to those whose writing tends to reflect the grammatical forms of certain dialects or the grammatical forms of nonnative speakers of English.
4. It does not include numerous lesson plans for teaching grammar to enrich and enhance writing. The list of references at the end of this chapter includes books that offer lesson ideas and teacher narratives about their own smart teaching of grammar.

What, then, *does* this book offer? The topics and potential benefits of this book are many:

1. It describes, in early chapters and/or in the Grammar Planner (Part 2), most of the grammatical concepts that most teachers might want to teach their students, from middle school through high school and possibly college.
2. It includes some descriptions of how other teachers—informed teachers who are also innovators and integrators—have experimented with teaching grammar more effectively, intertwined with writing.
3. It provides a rationale for what aspects of grammar—what constructions, what stylistic features—give you and your students the most effect for the least effort. This, too, is the less-is-more principle (Noguchi, 1991, p. 121).
4. It explains these concepts in sufficient detail to enable you to create your own lessons.
5. It offers a framework for teaching such key constructions throughout the process of creating a particular piece of writing and over the course of time.
6. It indicates what grammatical elements are tested most heavily on the ACT English test, which includes not only revising and editing sentences, but attending to the flow of paragraphs and whole pieces. My

informal analysis of six practice tests is more finely tuned than the overview of topics that the practice books offer, but my analysis is also, of course, more subjective.

7. It suggests guidelines for deciding what aspects of grammar to teach.

8. It offers an overview of grammatical concepts for enriching writing and for enhancing it through editing.

9. It includes a grammar overview (Part 2, the Grammar Planner) that provides a marginal column for recording instructional decisions about whether or when to teach the concept. This Planner can be used by individual teachers, teachers at a given grade level, or teachers across grade levels. It may also be used by language coordinators at local or state levels.

10. It ends with a scope-and-sequence chart that will help you easily keep track of which constructions you have chosen to teach and when and how you plan to teach—or have taught—them.

You are invited to leave those isolated grammar modules behind and join the ranks of other smart teachers who have started to experiment with ways of teaching grammar more effectively in order to help students enrich and enhance their writing. In *Grammar to Enrich and Enhance Writing*, I describe this approach as a "grammar of possibility" that is simultaneously positive, productive, and practical.

What do classroom teachers think? Rebecca Schipper, a ninth-grade teacher in the Hudsonville, Michigan, public school system, wrote in her journal about her experimentation and experiences in abandoning her usual grammar lessons and teaching three grammatical/stylistic devices for enriching writing:

> Well, it is February now, and the kids are using the "out-of-order" adjectives, appositives, and parallel constructions on their own! I am amazed that something has actually stuck with them. In past years, I have spent week after week working on comma rules and semicolons and teaching students the name of each rule. I didn't this year, and the funny thing is, the kids are using them better than before.
>
> One of my students, a special-ed student who struggles with writing (by his own admission, "hates this stupid writing crap") turned in a piece of writing two days ago that was the best writing he has ever done. I told him about it and he said, "Well, yeah, it was super easy." Guess what his paragraph was full of? Out-of-order adjectives, appositives, and parallel constructions.
>
> The misconception that exists among teachers (new and veteran) is that grammar must be taught with drill-and-practice activities. I am here to ask WHY? When research supports over and over again that the drill and practice doesn't work, and when things like Connie is showing do work, why would I ever go back to slowly boring kids

to death with drill and practice? I can't, on purpose, ever do that to them, when they (and research) have proven to me it doesn't work.

Consider me sold on the idea of intertwining grammar with writing.

Resources for the smart teacher of grammar, whether expert or novice

Background reading for the smart teaching of grammar

The National Council of Teachers of English (www.ncte.org) has published several resources:

NCTE. *Professional communities at work: Grammar.* (no date). This grammar kit is designed especially for teachers to use in a study group. The packet includes some "framing observations and questions," study group guidelines, Q&As about grammar, online grammar resources, a notebook for writers, eleven articles reprinted from NCTE journals, and the book *Grammar Alive!* (see Haussamen entry).

In the past decade or so, NCTE's journals have included several issues on teaching grammar, usually focusing on teaching grammar in the context of writing. These include *English Journal*, November 1996, January 2003, and May 2006; *Voices from the Middle*, March 2001; and *Language Arts*, July 2004. There may also be more recent issues.

Haussamen, B., with Benjamin, A.; Kolln, M.; & Wheeler, R. S. (2003). *Grammar Alive!* Urbana, IL: National Council of Teachers of English. This popular book includes, as one of its recommended goals, developing students' ability to analyze the grammatical structures of sentences. Mostly, however, the teacher vignettes focus on the *use* of grammatical constructions. This book is a valuable addition to the smart teacher's library of resources.

Schuster, E. (2003). *Breaking the rules: Liberating writers through innovative grammar instruction*. Portsmouth, NH: Heinemann–Boynton/Cook. Wonderfully informative, this book will change English teachers' perceptions of traditional grammar and of how published writers use and punctuate language. Broadly informed, it is illustrated with lively anecdotes and practical activities that will lead teachers to new insights about teaching grammar, writing, and style.

Weaver, C. (1996). *Teaching grammar in context*. Portsmouth, NH: Heinemann–Boynton/Cook. Especially strong on what to teach, what not to teach, and why.

Weaver, C. (Forthcoming). *Grammar to enrich and enhance writing*. Portsmouth, NH: Heinemann–Boynton/Cook. This book will include a section offering a perspective on how to teach (and how not to teach) grammar for writing; a section with examples and suggestions for teaching grammatical options and conventions; and a concluding section of teacher narratives about teaching editing and working with special populations.

Lesson ideas: Activities and teacher narratives

Noden, H. (1999). *Image grammar: Using grammatical structures to teach writing*. Portsmouth, NH: Heinemann–Boynton/Cook. An outstanding resource for smart teachers ready to experiment with teaching grammar to enrich writing, this book includes a CD with examples that can be printed for class use, sample pictures to stimulate writing, and links to useful Web pages with artwork.

Noden, H. (Forthcoming). *Image grammar activities book*. Logan, IA: Perfection Learning. This is an activities book—as opposed to a workbook—for students, to help them learn to paint with words by describing real-world images and imitating master writers. One section teaches fifteen of the twenty most common grammatical errors as proofreading/writing strategies. Another section introduces advanced image grammar techniques such as noun collages and grammatical brush strokes in combination. The book includes a teacher's manual with five PowerPoint presentations for classroom use.

Weaver, C. (Ed.). (1998). *Lessons to share: On teaching grammar in context*. Portsmouth, NH: Heinemann–Boynton/Cook. Includes articles by Tom Romano, Harry Noden, Don Killgallon, and several other classroom teachers on ways of incorporating grammar into writing instruction.

Weaver, C. (Forthcoming). *Grammar to enrich and enhance writing*. Portsmouth, NH: Heinemann–Boynton/Cook. Will include several chapters on how teachers are currently teaching grammar to strengthen writing—in conjunction with the writing process itself. See the preceding listing under "Background Reading for the Smart Teaching of Grammar" for a fuller description of the book.

Wheeler, R. S., & Swords, R. (2006). *Code-switching: Teaching standard English in urban classrooms*. Urbana, IL: National Council of Teachers of English. This book is a detailed look at successful methods the authors have described in articles in *English Journal* and *Language Arts*. In-depth background rationale is also provided.

Style

Christensen, F. (1967). *Notes toward a new rhetoric: Six essays for teachers*. New York: Harper & Row. This little book has inspired most of us who are currently writing books about teaching grammar to enrich writing, not just to correct "errors." For teachers with a reasonable background in grammar, this out-of-print book is still inspirational. After his death, Christensen's wife added three of his other essays to the book and published it as *Notes toward a new rhetoric: Nine essays for teachers* (1978, Harper & Row).

Williams, J. M. (2005). *Style: Ten lessons in clarity and grace* (8th ed.). New York: Pearson Education. On the inside cover appear Williams' ten principles for clarity and grace. Generations of serious writers have found this book helpful in using grammar more effectively. Teachers can draw upon these lessons to create minilessons of their own. A much smaller book setting forth Williams' ten lessons is his *Style: The basics of clarity and grace* (2003), published by Addison Wesley Longman. The larger book has not only more details but also larger print.

Sentence combining

Killgallon, D., & Killgallon, J. (2006). *Grammar for middle school: A sentence-composing approach*. Portsmouth, NH: Heinemann. This book on sentence composing includes four kinds of sentence-composing activities: sentence unscrambling to imitate; combining to imitate; imitating alone (using the structure of the model but with students' own content); and expanding without imitating. The sentences students work with are all derived from the writings of professionals. Fourteen kinds of grammatical constructions are covered, but terminology is not emphasized. Designed for student use.

Killgallon, D., & Killgallon, J. (Forthcoming). *Grammar for high school: A sentence-composing approach*. Portsmouth, NH: Heinemann.

Strong, W. (1994). *Sentence combining: A composing book* (3rd ed.). New York: McGraw-Hill. Without using grammatical terminology, Strong offers several units of open-ended sentence-combining activities that will naturally result in a variety of grammatical constructions, especially when students compare their differing results. One unit provides simple sentences derived from those of superb stylists and invites students to compare their sentence-combining results with the originals. One of the appendices includes minilessons on parallel structure, sentence variety, choosing effective sentences, paragraph organization, and paragraph "packaging." Designed for student use.

Strong, W. (1996). *Writer's toolbox: A sentence-combining workshop*. New York: McGraw-Hill. This book presents a workshop approach to writing, with sentence-combining, imitating, expanding, and revising exercises keyed to phases of the writing process. It also includes sections on "tools" of basic and advanced grammar, usage, and punctuation—all presented or elaborated through sentence combining.

Strong describes this book as "designed to help students build sentence and paragraph skills collaboratively by working together *in groups*" (p. xi; emphasis mine). Designed for student use.

Mechanics and punctuation

Anderson, J. (2005). *Mechanically inclined: Building grammar, usage, and style into writer's workshop*. Portland, ME: Stenhouse. Drawing primarily from his extensive experience teaching sixth grade, Anderson has provided "a treasure," as Vicki Spandel calls it in her foreword to the book. Spandel further writes, "This book is more than an overview of how to teach conventions, though. It's a modestly, beautifully presented book on how to teach, period." Having learned most of what I know about good teaching from elementary teachers, I second Spandel's praise and recommend this book to teachers at any level.

More on grammar itself

Gordon, K. E. (1993). *The deluxe transitive vampire: A handbook of grammar for the innocent, the eager, and the doomed*. New York: Knopf. This treatment of traditional grammar provides explanations and examples that will delight as well as inform.

Kolln, M. (2007). *Rhetorical grammar: Grammatical choices, rhetorical effects* (5th ed.). New York: Longman. This is a grammar book, no doubt about it, but the material on the effects of certain grammatical structures is what makes the book unique. The treatment of grammar reflects Kolln's grounding in linguistics. For the teacher who is seriously interested in studying grammar and its effects on listeners and readers.

Lester, M., & Beason, L. (2005). *The McGraw-Hill handbook of English grammar and usage*. New York: McGraw-Hill. Written by authors with background in linguistic descriptions of English, this handbook is nevertheless more traditional than otherwise, as are most of the linguistically informed books currently published. The book devotes nearly a hundred pages to basic grammar and is therefore an excellent resource for teachers who want more in-depth knowledge. Nearly two hundred pages are devoted to "how to find and correct mistakes."

Lunsford, A. *The everyday writer* (2004) and *The everyday writer online* (2005). Boston: Bedford/Saint Martin's. This linguistically informed text, designed for college writers, is moderately expensive in both the paper and online versions. The text describes the structure of English in some depth, with an overall focus on writing; an accompanying set of exercises is available. Lunsford has also published a more thorough and more expensive text, *St. Martin's Handbook 2003*, which comes with varying supplements (2005). A simpler, relatively inexpensive version is *Easy Writer: A Pocket Guide* (2005), which includes less information on grammar. All of these are published by Bedford/Saint Martin's.

Grammar/usage

The first two books emphasize "errors," which is not exactly a positive approach to grammar. However, they may serve as useful resources.

Beason, L., & Lester, M. (2006). *A commonsense guide to grammar and usage* (4th ed.). Boston, MA: Bedford/St. Martin's. Slightly over five hundred pages, this book provides everything teachers might want to know about grammar, usage, punctuation, and capitalization. Because of its thoroughness, the book is an excellent resource and reference tool for teachers.

Cazort, D. (1997). *Under the grammar hammer: The 25 most important grammar mistakes and how to avoid them* (2d ed.). Los Angeles: Lowell House. The humor, cartoons, and folksy style of this book make it easy to read and study. Highly useful for helping teachers learn the grammar they most need in order to help students edit, the book is suitable for students, too, from perhaps as early as middle school on up. The last chapter's subtitle recommends "America, Lighten Up."

Great Source Education Group. (no date). *Punctuation pockets*. Boston: Houghton Mifflin. These are file folders, three for different educational levels. Their covers and inside flaps include punctuation rules.

Hacker, D. (2003). *A writer's reference* (5th ed.). Boston: Bedford/St. Martin's. More than a grammar book, and more thorough in its treatment of grammatical errors than my book, Hacker's handbook may be just right for teachers' reference. Since it takes a rather conservative stance on usage, it may be useful in studying for standardized tests of English like those that are part of the ACT and SAT.

2 Teaching Grammar "an Inch Wide and a Mile Deep"

Theresa Reagan-Donk, coordinator of instruction for the Hudsonville, Michigan, public schools, talks about good teaching as being "an inch wide and a mile deep." She means that instead of trying to "cover" one thing after another, rapidly and superficially, we should teach fewer things but teach them deeply and well. Nowhere is this truer than in the teaching of grammar. Traditional grammar books try to cover everything, and teachers concerned with covering the grammar books have commonly found that students haven't learned much of anything well enough to apply it independently in their writing. That's the reason for the Grammar Planner (Part 2)—it's a place where you can indicate what you choose to teach, from among the many possibilities. Teaching *less* is one of the keys to instruction that makes a difference. But how can we teach less and do it more productively? The answer, in general, is to teach those few constructions and skills "a mile deep."

This chapter offers:

- An example of how Jeff Henderson and I taught participial phrases during a unit on folktales.
- A general framework for teaching key grammatical constructions and skills not only throughout one particular writing assignment but repeatedly over time.
- An example of how Rebecca Schipper's students spontaneously began using grammatical constructions they'd previously been taught.
- A demonstration by Jeff Anderson, classroom teacher and author of *Mechanically Inclined* (2005), of how he has taught certain editing skills to his sixth graders.

Teaching grammatical constructions during the writing process

Particularly in middle and secondary school classrooms, teachers often assign a specific writing topic and genre to the entire class, then lead students through the writing process, one phase after another. How can we teach grammatical options and skills in such classrooms? We are accustomed, perhaps, to teaching minilessons on the mechanics of writing when the need arises. But we are not all so accustomed to teaching the use of effective language structures when students' own writing provides the opportunity.

Consider the writing Amy produced in Scott Peterson's class in response to an assignment to write about a scary night. First, the students clustered ideas for their description, and Amy spontaneously came up with some *-ing* modifiers, two of which she incorporated in the following sentence: *I felt the wind* <u>*going through the trees*</u> *like ice cream* <u>*melting in the summer*</u> (Weaver 1996, p. 167). While the students wrote, Scott walked around the room, briefly answering students' questions and offering suggestions and praise. As he did, he might have noticed Amy's sentence, decided to write it on the board or on a transparency, and then presented a brief minilesson showing the class how they could add action phrases to their description. Though extremely brief, a minilesson like this offers other writers in the class a grammatical tool they may want to consciously employ.

In the ebb and flow of the writing process, there are many spontaneous opportunities to teach the use of modifying structures or parallelism or other grammatical constructions that might enhance the elaboration and flow of ideas. As students begin revising and editing, still more opportunities arise to teach effective ways of revising sentences and paragraphs, as well as editing skills like subject-verb agreement or the use of punctuation. Sometimes teachers don't preplan their minilessons other than to remind themselves to look for opportunities to teach a particular concept based on their students' writing that day. In other words, they plan to seize opportunities that arise from their students' writing.

Often, however, teachers have the greatest long-term effect by starting with a preplanned lesson on using a particular grammatical construction to express content effectively and then reemphasizing that same concept through the revising, editing, and proofreading processes. Of course, time constraints make it impossible to do this sort of teaching with every piece of assigned or self-chosen writing, and even when we try our best, some aspect of the process may get shortchanged: usually either revising or editing. When that happens, we can make a note to be sure to emphasize the missing step next time.

That said, here's a look at one attempt to do it all. The story is still being played out.

In the ebb and flow of the writing process, there are many spontaneous opportunities to teach grammatical constructions that might enhance the elaboration and flow of ideas.

The Paper Bag Princess and participial phrases

Jeff Henderson, a sixth-grade teacher at Baldwin Middle School in Hudsonville, Michigan, asked me to teach a demonstration lesson on using present participial phrases, specifically the kind that offer "extra" information to enrich writing: ones that have to be "set off" by commas. As

Jeff said, "Such sentences represent what most sixth-grade students already consider to be good sentences. So your instruction will awaken their awareness to what a sentence can become when *-ing* phrases are used." Since Jeff and I had been working on tying grammatical instruction in writing to the literature Jeff used in the classroom, I volunteered to develop a lesson relating to his current unit on folktales.

After explaining that the students would be writing either a prequel or a sequel to *The Paper Bag Princess* (Munsch, 1980), I then read the brief text while showing the illustrations on the overhead. In this spoof of the usual fairy tale plot, the prince is saved from the dragon by the princess, who is clothed only in a paper bag because the dragon has burned down her castle. After a brief class discussion—it turned out that most of the students were familiar with the story—I then presented some participial phrases as examples, calling them simply *-ing* phrases. The following were my most successful examples, drawn from the prequel to *The Paper Bag Princess* that I had written and would later share as a model (see Figure 2–1):

Tall and willowy, Princess Elizabeth had brown hair with blond highlights and clear blue eyes, <u>penetrating to the very heart of all who knew her.</u>

Ellie was adventurous, too, <u>riding into the dense forest at every opportunity,</u> <u>looking for new things like hidden pools or caves.</u>

<u>Riding forth one sunny day,</u> <u>passing from the safety of the castle yard into the uncertainty of the forest,</u> Ellie heard a mournful howl.

After asking what each *-ing* phrase described, I pointed out that all the phrases added interesting "extra" details about the princess and her actions and therefore needed to be set off from the rest of the sentence by a comma or commas. We then considered whether either of the *-ing* phrases in the middle example could logically be moved to the front of the sentence; generally, we liked the idea of moving the first *-ing* phrase to the front: *Riding into the dense forest at every opportunity, Ellie was adventurous, too, looking for new things like hidden pools or caves.*

After leading the students in creating some *-ing* phrases together and deciding whether they were movable or not, I finally invited them to work in pairs to add details via *-ing* phrases to some bare-bones sentences I had developed about the prince and about the dragon. (I suggested this would generate ideas for the students' own writing.) The skeletal sentences included these:

The prince stared at the paper bag princess.

The dragon smashed the castle.

As the students shared ideas and wrote, Jeff and I walked around the room, helping the students grasp the concept of adding an *-ing* phrase at

Princess Elizabeth's Adventure

Princess Elizabeth, known as Ellie by family and friends, was beautiful. Tall and willowy, she had brown hair with blonde highlights and clear blue eyes, <u>penetrating to the very heart of all who knew her</u>, attracting everyone whose path she crossed. Ellie was adventurous, too, <u>riding into the dense forest at every opportunity</u>, <u>looking for new things like hidden pools or caves</u>.

<u>Riding forth one sunny day</u>, passing from the safety of the castle yard into the uncertainty of the forest, Ellie heard a mournful howl. She halted abruptly, <u>wondering what could possibly be crying so pitifully</u>. Ellie thought perhaps she shouldn't venture alone into the darker and darker forest, yet curiosity and concern led her on, <u>hoping she could somehow ease the creature's pain</u>. As Ellie rode among strange kinds of bushes and trees, their branches closer and closer, the creature's plight sounded more and more desperate. Finally Ellie came to a small clearing, where a beautiful fox, silver with a bushy tail, lay trapped. <u>Yowling and moaning</u>, the fox looked at her desperately, <u>pleading with pain-filled eyes for her to free him from his pain</u>. Carefully, Ellie dismounted, <u>tying her horse's reins around the nearest tree so he wouldn't run from the fox</u>. Fearful but determined, Ellie stepped on the edge of the trap, pulled on the top of the metal jaws that clamped the fox's foot, and gently released that foot, mangled and torn from his efforts to escape the trap. The two of them stood looking at each other, fox and princess, Ellie's eyes filling with tears of relief and the fox's with tears of gratitude.

The fox was so grateful that when his paw had healed, he told the other forest creatures how the girl had rescued him. Eventually, word reached her parents and others in the castle and town.

From then on, Princess Elizabeth was known fondly as Ellie the Brave.

FIGURE 2–1. My prequel, written as a model

©2007 by Constance Weaver, from *The Grammar Plan Book* (Heinemann: Portsmouth, NH).

the beginning or end of the sentence to modify "the prince" or "the dragon." We also pointed out when the writers needed to set off their *-ing* phrases with a comma.

After that, I shared the prequel that I'd written the night before, in which I'd used *-ing* phrases and "out-of-order" adjectives (see Chapter 3); Jeff had already taught the students to experiment with these in their writing. I pointed out again that all my *-ing* phrases occurred at the beginning or end of the sentence but in either case described the subject—just the way published writers most often use and place such modifiers. At the end of the class period came the follow-up assignment: Write a prequel or sequel to *The Paper Bag Princess* using some participial phrases (at least two) to make the writing come alive, to show instead of tell.

The following day, Jeff taught the lesson to his other classes. He also looked at the draft prequels and sequels that students in the classes I had taught were writing. Jeff explained:

> Noting many misconceptions, I put the overhead transparency back up and reviewed with the students what you had underlined in your story. The students asked some general questions, and then I had them "peer edit," looking for use of the *-ing* phrases and helping each other make corrections.

There were still quite a few wrong ideas, misunderstandings about how participial phrases worked. As Jeff described it, "There were two main problems: (1) Students misunderstood that the goal was to modify the subject noun, and (2) they also misunderstood that what we wanted them to create was entire participial phrases, not just single-word participles." In class we had looked at and created only *-ing phrases*, not single-word participles, because I was aiming for greater development of the ideas. Obviously I had not managed to make that clear, nor had Jeff and I done so when we walked around the room while students were expanding the sentences about the prince and the dragon.

In the days that followed, while the students were drafting their stories, Jeff did another minilesson to help clarify what these "nonessential," extra *-ing* phrases looked like and how they could be constructed to tell more about the subject of a sentence. He also taught a lesson differentiating the kind of phrases we'd taught from other uses of verb forms ending in *-ing*.

Two of the best student pieces are shown in Figures 2–2 and 2–3. I have underlined the nonessential participial *-ing* phrases in each piece. Nate's piece (Figure 2–2) has only one set-off participial phrase but generously includes single-word participles that occur before the noun: *frightening*, *crunching* (probably an adjectival), *tiring*, *flaming*, and *swirling*. This may have been the result of not understanding that we were aiming for entire participial phrases and/or confusion stemming from the lesson Jeff taught to help students grasp what we wanted. We simply do not know the cause or causes, but we do know that Nate was not the only student whose use of *-ing* phrases wasn't entirely what we had anticipated.

Drake the Dragon

This is the story of how the dragon became the smartest and most fierce dragon in the land.

Once upon a time, there was a dragon named Drake. Drake attended the College of Dragon Training (C.D.T.) but the problem was, he was the very worst dragon there. While other students were burning down entire forests in one fiery breath, Drake could barely set fire to a twig. He was also constantly picked on by the C.D.T. bullies, the frightening, ferocious Fire Wings.

Drake was also different in other ways. For example, he had an appetite for castles, princesses, and princes instead of crunching, hot charcoal.

One day on his way to flight class, Drake unfortunately crossed paths with the Fire Wings. "Gonna take eighty tiring, slow days to fly around the world again?" one teased. Another pulled a toothpick out of his back pocket and asked, "Hey, could you do me a favor and burn this up? Or is it too much for you?" <u>Laughing hysterically</u>, the gruesome group casually strolled away.

That was the final straw for Drake. He gathered up every last bit of his energy and blew out a flaming, swirling fire-ball. It not only fried the toothpick, but charred the Fire Wings as well. From that day on, Drake was never picked on again.

He kept on practicing with his newly found strength. Eventually he could fly around the world in ten seconds and burn down one hundred forests in one blow.

From then on Drake was known as the smartest and fiercest dragon in the land.

FIGURE 2–2. Nate's story "Drake the Dragon"

Did everything go smoothly? Obviously not, either for Jeff or for me—and you don't know all of it yet! At the last moment, I discovered that I'd left some transparencies at home, and Jeff had to make new ones. Thrown off balance by this final scramble, I forgot to set the stage for what the students in that first class were going to do: I neglected to say right away that they would be writing a prequel or sequel to *The Paper Bag Princess* so they could be alert for ideas as they listened to me read the book and looked at the illustrations on the overhead. How could I have forgotten something so obvious? One of my examples didn't work well with the first class, and one of the bare-bones sentences about the prince and the dragon was harder to add *-ing* phrases to than I had anticipated. During the days when students were drafting their stories, Jeff had surgery on his knee and was unable to give the students feedback on their stories as quickly as he would have liked. Does all of this sound like normal teaching? It was!

Walking bravely and independently into the sunset, Princess Elizabeth thought long and hard about how the wealthy, unkind prince had betrayed her. She learned that a true prince should be a loving, kind hearted young man who truly cares about others. A true prince shows good character through his inner self. She did not need a prince to take care of her. Thinking independently, Princess Elizabeth decided to start her own business. With her caring personality, she made paper bag clothing and apparel for the poor and homeless.

One day, a poor man came into her shop. The man, desperate for clothing to wear, asked her to make a paper bag outfit for him. He thanked the princess for her generosity and left the store. The man, visiting often, was given more and more paper bag clothing made by the Princess. The princess was always willing to make him more clothing.

At the time, Princess Elizabeth didn't know the man was more than just her friend. Although he was a poor man dressed in paper bag clothing, his heart was always overflowing with kindness. Lovingly, the princess measured the size of his heart rather than his appearance.

Looking deeply into her eyes, the man asked Princess Elizabeth to marry him. The princess had never, in her life, met someone so thoughtful. Responding willingly with a "yes," she saw the poor man transform suddenly into a handsome prince. Amazingly, this did not surprise the princess, for this is what she saw in his heart all along. Princess Elizabeth was a queen to be!

Their wedding took place a few months later. Princess Elizabeth, walking happily down the aisle, was wearing a brown paper bag wedding gown. Gazing at the prince who was waiting for her, wearing a paper bag tuxedo, she was thinking how lucky she was for realizing there was more to a boy than his charm. Princess Elizabeth realized that her Prince was truly more wonderful than anyone else on Earth.

Continuing giving to the poor, Queen Elizabeth and her handsome husband took good care of the people in their kingdom. Helping to make paper bag clothing for the needy were their four caring and giving children.

Living happily ever after, they were blissfully blessed.

FIGURE 2–3. Hannah's sequel about Princess Elizabeth

Despite everything, Jeff estimates that about 40 percent of the students used this "new" grammatical construction to add details to their stories, and some of the resultant prequels and sequels were excellent.

As we talked about the results of our teaching, we wondered whether more groundwork should have been laid with a simpler assignment than the prequel or sequel. Should I have first asked the students to write just a paragraph in which they used two participial phrases? Maybe. Well, probably. On the other hand, Jeff and I both knew that one pass through the writing process would not be enough, no matter what we did. Jeff brought up an article about learning words, in which the authors reported that children required eight to ten repetitions of a concept before it was learned (Miller & Gildea, 1991). So we shouldn't be surprised that even our multiple attempts weren't yet enough for all the students.

As I write, Jeff is headed for another round of surgery but says that afterward, "I will re-visit this grammar concept and see what nine or ten iterations brings!" We both wait to see what long-term effects this teaching may have.

Framework for teaching grammar throughout the writing process

In planning extended teaching of grammatical concepts, it helps to have a framework—steps you can use as reminders of what can make such teaching finally take hold and become part of students' own repertoire as writers. Here is my current version of such a framework, which I keep in mind as I plan but often modify in practice:

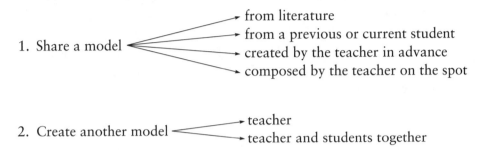

1. Share a model
   - from literature
   - from a previous or current student
   - created by the teacher in advance
   - composed by the teacher on the spot

2. Create another model
   - teacher
   - teacher and students together

3. Compose (or do a related activity) in small groups or pairs; share and clarify as needed.
4. Compose a sentence or sentences individually; share. Teacher can check the work if desired and possible.
5. Ask students to apply concept—that is, to use the grammatical element or writing skill—in their own writing.
6. Consider giving students a checklist that includes the item, to use in their final revision or editing phase.
7. Provide for feedback from peers and/or provide teacher feedback.
8. Teach a new minilesson and/or hold revising or editing conferences to reteach a concept as needed, showing students how to apply (or correctly apply) the concept in their own writing.
9. If needed, go through the process again with a different piece of writing. At the very least, continue helping students apply this concept as they revise and/or edit other pieces of writing.

Let me repeat: This is not a sequence set in stone, but simply a reminder of steps that can make the learning and application of the construction or skill more effective. What you *need* to do depends on your classes, no two of which ever seem to be the same; what you *can* do depends partly, perhaps, on whether or not you can take to heart the idea of teaching fewer concepts but teaching them more effectively.

I echo Theresa Reagan-Donk's advice to teach an inch wide and a mile deep. Decide what aspects of grammar are really worth teaching and then teach them well throughout the production of one piece of writing and over the following weeks, as needed—indeed, over the rest of the school year as you continue to show students how to revise their writing for greater effectiveness. The lessons take a while to prepare, but you can build a repertoire over time, share lesson plans among colleagues, and borrow appropriate literary examples and teaching ideas from elsewhere.

Grammar lessons applied spontaneously

The ultimate goal, of course, is for students to take what we've taught them and use it independently and spontaneously, without our having to prompt them—either by teaching a reminder lesson or developing a revising or editing checklist that specifies using the concept or skill. Rebecca Schipper, a ninth-grade teacher in Jeff's school system, has had great success this year teaching

- "adjectives out of order" (a term from Harry Noden's *Image Grammar*),
- appositives, and
- parallel grammatical constructions

for students to use in their writing. The lessons were taught in that order.

For the lesson on parallelism, Rebecca first read the students David Bouchard's picture book *If You're Not from the Prairie . . .* (1993). Her assignment sheet (see Figure 2–4) asks students to write a paragraph using the book as a model. It does not specifically ask them to use out-of-order adjectives or appositives, which Rebecca had previously taught, though it does say, "Remember the stylistic devices we have used." Several students did include the previously taught constructions, as we can see in the following examples.

> If you're not the youngest child you don't know what it's like to have an older sibling, whome with you always fight. If you're not the youngest child, you don't know what it's like to have your parents, caring and clueless, on your side. If you're not the youngest child you don't know what it's like to watch your older brother, a towering goof-ball, getting all the privileges. If you're not the youngest child you don't know what it's like to love your big brother with all your might.
>
> —Brooke Zitricki

Of course, the "if" clauses copy the parallel construction in the model, but Brooke's paper also includes out-of-order adjectives—*caring and clueless*—and an appositive, *a towering goof-ball*.

In the following piece, Kara, too, has used adjectives out of order—*weak and vulnerable*—and an appositive, *a sly and tricky eel*. Her "if" clauses are similar to Brooke's:

Stylistic Devices

So far, we have discussed two ways to improve your writing stylistically. Those two ways were through the use of "out of order" adjectives and appositives. A third way is through the use of **parallelism**, also known as **parallel structure**.

Simply put, parallelism is using the same structure (for emphasis) to list things. You are probably familiar with this idea from working with comma rules. Below are some examples of parallelism from Elie Wiesel's *Night* (1960).

> Several days passed. Several weeks. Several months. Life had returned to normal. A wind of calmness and reassurance blew through our houses. <u>The traders were doing good business</u>, <u>the students lived buried in their books</u>, and <u>the children played in the streets</u>. (p. 4)

> <u>The Germans were already in the town</u>, <u>the Fascists were already in power</u>, <u>the verdict had already been pronounced</u>, yet the Jews of Signet continued to smile. (pp. 7–8)

> We were no longer allowed <u>to go into restaurants or cafes</u>, <u>to travel on the railway</u>, <u>to attend the synagogue</u>, <u>to go out into the street after six o'clock</u>. (p. 9)

> One by one they passed in front of me, teachers, friends, others, all those I had been afraid of, all those I once could have laughed at, all those I had lived with over the years. They went by, fallen, <u>dragging their packs</u>, <u>dragging their lives</u>, <u>deserting their homes</u>, the years of their childhood, <u>cringing like beaten dogs</u>. (pp. 14–15)

What other, unmarked examples of parallelism do you find in the above sentences?

Now, find two examples of parallelism in the novel you are reading. Try to look only in the reading for this week. Write the examples (along with the page numbers) in the space below.

YOUR ASSIGNMENT: After reading *If You're Not from the Prairie*, the picture book story, write a paragraph of your own choosing using the same format. Pick something that is specific to you and then elaborate. Remember the stylistic devices we have used earlier, and now, parallel structure. Be sure to use an interesting opener and closer, good word choice, MLA format, and any other writing requirements we have covered.

FIGURE 2–4. Rebecca Schipper's assignment on parallelism

©2007 by Constance Weaver, from *The Grammar Plan Book* (Heinemann: Portsmouth, NH).

If you're not an only child, you don't know what it's like, to have no brothers and sisters, and not to have to fight. If you're not an only child, you can't know, you won't know, that you don't have to share, and if you want anything, just give your parents a little glare. If you're not an only child, you're definitely not spoiled, you don't have people, weak and vulnerable, wrapped around your finger in a coil.

If you're not an only child, a sly and tricky eel, you will never know how it feels.

—Kara Petkus

Here is Caleb's response to the same assignment:

Fierce Lion

If you don't wrestle, you don't know what it's like, you can't know what it's like. Wrestling for a team brings a sense of focus, adrenaline, anger, pain, sweat, and hate for your opponent and all of these emotions pulse through your body with great intensity.

If you don't get a takedown, you don't know what it's like, you can't know what it's like. The feeling of accomplishment and weakness. The slam between two huge masses of muscle. The state of being on top and smashing the opponents face into the mat. You can see his pain, anguish, frustration, and blood pouring out of his body in one great emotion. If you were a wrestler, twisted and tormented, you would also feel no compassion for your contender.

If you don't get pinned, you don't know what it's like, you can't know what it's like. The feeling of defeat, disappointment, and dissatisfaction. The feeling that settles in you when you let your team down, your family down, your home crowd, and other loved ones in your life down.

If you don't wrestle, you don't know me, you can't throw me. I am a wrestler, a fierce lion on the hunt, on the mat it can be seen. In mental silence generating a deep-seated mean.

—Caleb Schutter

Notice that the last "If you don't . . ." construction does not end the same as the others. Caleb breaks the pattern to bring his piece to an end. Notice too that there is parallelism in his use of effective sentence fragments and within the fragments themselves. He also uses *twisted and tormented* as out-of-order adjectives, as well as a metaphorical appositive: *I am a wrestler, a fierce lion on the hunt*. Clearly Caleb is a skilled writer, with command of a growing repertoire of grammatical options for conveying ideas and details and figurative language.

From the first lesson on, Rebecca began noticing that her students were using the taught structures spontaneously in their other writing. Her December 6 journal entry states:

> Every week my students have a quiz over their novel reading. The really fun thing is that on these essay quizzes, the kids are using "out-of-order" adjectives and appositives without my ever prompting them to include these. The students are just starting to get it that these kinds of additions to sentences really add a lot. Shockingly, I haven't seen much overuse of it either.

In February, Rebecca reiterated that kids were still using out-of-order adjectives and appositives on their own, along with parallel constructions.

No wonder she is "sold" on the idea of teaching an inch wide and a mile deep!

Teaching editing over time

As teachers, we often despair of teaching editing skills successfully. Will students ever really learn, much less apply, what we teach? In the following narrative Jeff Anderson, sixth-grade teacher at Rayburn Middle School and adjunct professor at Trinity University in San Antonio, Texas, demonstrates that less is more in teaching editing: that it's better to teach editing, too, an inch wide and a mile deep. His book *Mechanically Inclined* (2005) contains many such narratives and over thirty specific lessons on how to teach grammar and mechanics with mentor texts and inquiry-based lessons. He begins with some general observations about teaching editing.

Editing instruction: Where's the error?

It's the second week of school. I put a sentence on the overhead and ask a student to read it aloud. "Tell me what you notice," I say to the class. They know the game; the sentence has something wrong with it. Immediately, Michael homes in on things that must be wrong: apostrophes, capitalization, commas. The problem is, the sentence is completely correct—a model, in fact. However, my new students believe that if a teacher asks them to look at a sentence, something must be wrong with it, and they need to pounce quickly. Grammar is a "gotcha" and mechanics are mistakes. Students are incredulous when I explain that there aren't any mistakes. I just want to hear what they observe.

Though the red pen has been put away by many teachers, red-pen thinking still marks the approach in most English classrooms, as do grammar and test-preparation materials. Where's the error? It's all about the error. What's wrong with that?

Effective editing instruction is more about teaching students the patterns and concepts of the English language that readers expect courteous writers to follow.

First, getting students to edit well is not primarily about practicing editing. Effective editing instruction is more about teaching students the patterns and concepts of the English language that readers expect courteous writers to follow. Rules. Mechanics. Grammar. Whatever you want to call it, readers seem to get in a tizzy if writers are so careless as not to edit their work. Thus, we try to teach kids to get in a tizzy about errors—and we all just end up in one big tizzy, pulled under by the constant undertow of errors. Some students simply give up and err with abandon. For the most part, kids know there is probably something wrong with their writing. They just don't know what it is or how to fix it.

For example, we do a good job of getting our students in a tizzy about the *it's* versus *its* problem, or *you're* versus *your*, or *their* versus *there* or *they're*. Students basically guess, and they get it right part of the time. It's easy to get young writers to the point where they know they should worry about their *there*s and *they're*s—but that's where it stops. This all reminds me of my dear mom's birthday. It fell on February 6 or 7. I knew it really hurt her feelings when I got it wrong—but I just knew I must be wrong, whatever day I thought it was. I never came up with a way to know the difference. That's how students make editing decisions. It's not about writing process or meaning. It becomes about "Yeah, I know this is where I mess up."

That's a start—awareness is a first step toward successful editing—but here is where most editing instruction runs astray, in my opinion. Instruction stays stuck in "catch them if you can." There are so many errors that teachers only need to cast out a net to catch plenty. Writing is no longer about creating meaning, shaping prose, making points clear. Writing seems to be about avoiding being wrong. We all hate being wrong, don't we?

If we teach a few editing skills, students may become slightly better editors with time—but not substantially better. On the other hand, if we have students edit sentences day after day after day, they will see editing as something divorced from the writing process, something they do so the teacher has time to take roll and is able to record an easy grade every week. That's not exactly the message I want to send either.

The solution? Don't give students sentences day after day with errors that they correct. That's not teaching editing—that's practicing. Practicing cycling can help me improve; however, if I practice improperly, I can be injured. Anyone who's ever tried to wrangle a class of students into finding errors and explaining why they think the constructions *are* errors has surely felt injured—even if the injury is only to the ego. Where on earth did they get that explanation? Did they pull it out of the sky? Students don't learn how to write correctly from merely editing strings of sentences. They learn within the writing process. They learn from studying powerful examples from the books they like: imitating, trying, playing with, and yes, editing for the most important concepts.

However, I can't stop at showing great sentences to kids and asking what they notice. I need to build on the knowledge they're gleaning by helping them generate their own sentences and edit their own and others' writing for important concepts like compound sentences and how to create them. Understanding compound sentences helps students avoid comma splices and add depth and connection to their ideas.

Not Compound Sentences	Compound Sentences
I studied for my test.	I was hitting Edwin and Ozzy, but they moved away from me.
I am so tired.	
I like apples and peaches.	I am mad so leave me alone.
My mom said I had to choose the skirt or the jeans. I couldn't have both.	My dog is very fat, but he is a fast runner.
Denamel and Miguel are my friends.	Alaina acts nice, but she's really evil.
	Furbie is cute and playful, but he poops all over the place.

FIGURE 2–5. Categorizing compound and noncompound sentences

Imitating

I start my lesson on compound sentences by introducing the coordinating conjunctions: *for, and, nor, but, or, yet, so* (FANBOYS). After chanting them a few times, I say, "I am going to show you a powerful tool for your writing that is going to help you write better and help you on writing tests." I want them to start off by knowing they already have fluency with the FANBOYS, so I ask them to write a sentence in their writer's notebook that uses one of the FANBOYS. I write my sentence on the overhead: *I love teaching, but I wish I made more money.* Some look at my model, some write. We share what we came up with. As we do, I record sentences on the board under two headings: *Not Compound Sentences* (on the left) and *Compound Sentences* (on the right), as shown in Figure 2–5.

"They're all good sentences, right?" I pause. "But what makes the two categories different?"

Samantha says, "One side is compound, the other's not."

"What do you notice about the compound sentences?" I take a few minutes, eliciting responses, shaping them around the fact that a compound sentence is two sentences combined together to show a connection. "Like compound words, they are put together. What do you notice about how they are joined?" I lead students back to the FANBOYS connectors if they don't notice them on their own.

The next day, I put up a few models from literature on the overhead and share a graphic depicting how a compound sentence is structured (see Figure 2–6). We talk about how we can tell if a sentence is compound or not. I share with them these checkpoints:

- Are there two sentences joined with one of the FANBOYS and a comma?
- Did you do a test to make sure each side of the compound sentence had a subject and verb? (Who or what did, or is, something? What did they do, or what are they?)

Use a comma and a **conjunction** to join sentences.

Sentence ,
*f*or
*a*nd
*n*or
*b*ut
*o*r
*y*et
*s*o
sentence .

FIGURE 2–6 Compound sentence patterns (From Anderson, 2005, p. 164. Used with permission.)

For many students, visuals and examples are more powerful teachers than rules.

Five Ways to Make Editing a Positive Experience

1. Spend more time highlighting what is right and beautiful than hunting for errors.

2. Make grammar about meaning. There is a purpose for the marks we use, and writers are responsible for knowing why they do what they do. Then, sometimes, we can break the rules.

3. Constantly write and collect and refer back to literature and students' own writing.

4. Teach concepts and patterns with visuals and examples.

5. Do express-lane edits.

• Are the ideas connected or related in some way?

Hunting and categorizing

After applying these questions to the model sentences on the overhead, we go back to our chart from the day before and apply the questions to those sentences. Then I ask them to find compound sentences in their reading and collect them in their writer's notebook, on cards, or on large wall charts (Anderson, 2005). As you might guess, several of the sentences will be wrong—a quick assessment of sorts—but this is not a failure. It merely lets you see where students are with the concept (Vygotsky, 1986). For example, when learning about compound sentences, students often find just any sentence with a FANBOY or a comma and think it's a compound. That's one of the steppingstones on the pathway, one step closer to the truth of compound sentences.

Another way to provide meaningful practice is to decombine sentences from literature and ask the students to recombine them. I also ask students to write one sentence about a read-aloud or any silent reading they've done. They can write sentences in their notebooks or on tiny strips of paper that can be given to me as they exit the classroom (Yoshida, 1985).

Discussing and clarifying

As the need arises, discussions should be held around the meaning of each of the FANBOYS. Students can then go back and search for more examples. Sometimes I type up the "found" compounds and have students cut them up and categorize them into compound and noncompound sentences. We repeat the discussion. Then students glue their compounds under the visual scaffold (Figure 2–6) in their writer's notebook. This way students have a ready supply of examples to refer back to. For many students, visuals and examples are more powerful teachers than rules.

Now that we've imitated, hunted, categorized, discussed, and clarified—and done the whole routine more than once—I can cue students to combine some of their own sentences so they can see how we use compound sentences as writers. I can also demonstrate how we as writers check our own work for what we call comma splices—commas joining two sentences without the presence of one of the FANBOYS.

We do need to practice editing frequently once a concept has started taking hold, but we practice with students' own writing. In my classroom, I like to do an "express-lane" edit (Anderson, 2005), based on the metaphor of the express lane at the grocery store, which we use when we have only a few items. We know that focused editing experiences (Spandel, 2005) are the most powerful, so why not pick only one or two items to look for? For example, we do a quick reread of a free-write and look for compound sentences or comma splices. (If students say they don't have any compound sentences, I tell them to add one.) Besides asking students to correct the errors they find in their writing, I also have them highlight instances when a concept is used correctly, by circling or underlining or by recording a reflection at the end of the draft. Afterward, we share the successes, errors, and stumbling blocks and problem-solve together.

How do we avoid teaching everything and nothing?

Here's the deal. When it comes to grammar and mechanics, we probably can't teach it all without deluging students with so much information they

1. Missing comma after an introductory element
2. Vague pronoun reference
3. Missing comma in a compound sentence
4. Wrong word
5. Missing comma(s) with a nonrestrictive element
6. Wrong or missing verb ending
7. Wrong or missing preposition
8. Comma splice
9. Missing or misplaced possessive apostrophe
10. Unnecessary shift in tense
11. Unnecessary shift in pronoun
12. Sentence fragment
13. Wrong tense or verb form
14. Lack of subject-verb agreement
15. Missing comma in a series
16. Lack of agreement between pronoun and antecedent
17. Unnecessary comma(s) with a restrictive element
18. Fused sentence
19. Misplaced or dangling modifier
20. *Its/It's* confusion

FIGURE 2–7. Twenty errors most commonly marked by college teachers (From Connors & Lunsford, 1988, as included in Lunsford, 2003, p. 14. Used with permission.)

remember nothing. So we need to go very deep with fewer concepts. Does it matter that my students are only sixth graders? Yes and no. Yes, because teaching editing concepts and guiding the editing process takes more time. No, in that the same or similar techniques work well with all levels of students. As teachers we know we have to focus first on what's important. I start by looking at the kinds of errors my students make, but to ground me I also like using Connors and Lunsford's 1988 study of the twenty errors most commonly marked by college teachers of writing (they're listed in Figure 2–7). Instead of falling into a big black hole of errors, I can handle twenty. And not only are these the ones featured on the state tests in Texas, where I live, but they may also have had significant influence on the relative weighting of editing issues on the ACT (see Chapter 5).

Moving away from red-pen thinking and error hunting (Weaver, 1996) takes time. I constantly have to temper my desire to show children all their errors when they show me something they are so very proud of. I think of the song "Cruel to Be Kind," by Nick Lowe. Some members of our profession think that marking up a student's draft is the medicine they need to become good writers: tough love, if you will. I am cruel now, they reason, but this will translate into kind later. At the other extreme, if I am only kind—"Domingo, this is so good"—and I never help him refine or hone his grammar and mechanics, though I may be kind in the moment, I am cruel for his future. So, avoiding both red-pen and hands-off thinking, I make my class about discovery, models, beauty, categorization, visuals, and writers using grammar and mechanics to shape text and create meaning. Then my students become the ones editing their writing, with instruction and guidance: They are both the writers and the editors.

Modifiers to Enrich Writing

3 ❧

At the end of the first session of Grammar in the Teaching of Writing, a course for prospective and practicing teachers, I introduced an activity designed to convince them that they knew, in practical terms, a lot more grammar than they thought they did.

First, I put on the overhead a copy of a sentence from Francis Christensen's *Notes Toward a New Rhetoric* (1967, pp. 12–13):

> The swells move rhythmically toward us, irregularly faceted, sparkling, growing taller and more powerful until the shining crest bursts, a transparent sheet of pale green water spilling over the top, breaking into blue-white foam as it cascades down the front of the wave, piling up in a frothy mound that the diminishing wave pushes up against the pilings, with a swishsmash, the foam drifting back, like a lace fan opened over the shimmering water as the spent wave returns whispering to the sea.

I asked students to listen and watch as I read the sentence from capital to period: How many complete "sentences" does it contain? Most students realized it is only one sentence, grammatically speaking. Then I put up another transparency, showing, as Christensen did, the levels of modification within the sentence, how it goes from one phrase to another modifying phrase to another subsidiary modifier, a true *cumulative* sentence that accumulates one detail after another as it goes:

1 The swells move rhythmically toward us,
  2 irregularly faceted,
  2 sparkling,
  2 growing taller and more powerful until the shining crest bursts,
    3 a transparent sheet of pale green water spilling over the top,
      4 breaking into blue-white foam as it cascades down the front of the wave,
      4 piling up in a frothy mound that the diminishing wave pushes up against the pilings,
        5 with a swishsmash,
      4 the foam drifting back,
        5 like a lace fan opened over the shimmering water as the spent wave returns whispering to the sea.

After quickly demonstrating how some of the modifiers refer back to a less deeply embedded line or word, I made the assignment: Start with a simple sentence, like *The car appeared at the horizon* or *The girl sat lazily on the dock*, and write a sentence that goes on and on, with each detail relating to something before it. I left the model projected on the screen but encouraged the class not to follow it slavishly: Just let go and write. (Try this yourself and see what happens!)

Before the next class period, I put some of the students' sentences on transparencies so I could point out the grammatical constructions they had used, even though most members of the class did not know the grammatical names. Point made, I think: We do not need to be able to name the grammatical constructions we use in order to use them effectively.

Whenever I assign this exercise, the class, collectively, uses all (or almost all) of the kinds of modifiers explained in this chapter. Why teach the different kinds of modifiers, then? Because many of us can learn to use the constructions more often and more effectively if we are more conscious of the possibilities. Think of the basics of a sentence as a cake without any filling and the modifiers as the filling that makes the cake especially delicious.

We teachers often find ourselves helping students use more precise nouns, or naming words, and more lively verbs, or action words: These are the most basic parts of the "cake." Precise nouns and lively verbs can, indeed, greatly strengthen a piece of writing. What makes the greatest difference, though, the "filling," is using modifiers to add detail, voice/style, and sentence variety/fluency—not just single-word modifiers but groups of words functioning together as a modifier. Do you need to "know grammar" first? Not really. I often hear teachers in one of my workshops say something like, "I don't know grammar, I can't teach grammar, but I can do THIS!"

This chapter includes basic grammatical concepts and terms for understanding how modifiers enrich sentences and for grasping some basic editing skills, both of which need to be taught to help students achieve their full potential as writers. (I've included a few minor terms as well to expand your understanding and confidence and to help you navigate more detailed grammar books.) It is not necessary to grasp all the concepts and terms now, but certain ones are important background for the rest of this chapter and the next: *noun, pronoun, nominal; verb, verb phrase; adjective, adjectival; adverb, adverbial; subject* plus *predicate; clause;* and *phrase.*

Do you need to "know grammar" first? Not really. I often hear teachers in one of my workshops say something like, "I don't know grammar, I can't teach grammar, but I can do THIS!"

Traditional and linguistic descriptions of the language

It's handy to have labels for the things we want to talk about. As children, we learn labels like *Mommy, Daddy, doggie, chair, car, tummy,* and a rapidly increasing array of other things. As we get older, we learn new sets of terms, like *steering wheel, dashboard, tires, gas tank* (and perhaps some of the parts under the hood of a car as well). We learn basic parts of the body, such as *tummy, eyes, arms, legs,* and gradually increase our knowledge of body parts, including internal organs like *heart, stomach* (not the same as "tummy"), and so on. We learn new concepts and terms as we need them.

So it is with certain aspects of language: We teachers need some basic terms in order to talk about using language effectively in writing, and you will need some background in grammar in order to comprehend parts of this book. Though research shows it's seldom helpful to have students analyze a sentence and label all its parts, it *is* helpful for teachers to be able to use a few grammatical terms in discussing examples of language use with students—labels are a kind of shorthand. This means that it's helpful if students, too, are familiar with a few basic grammatical terms.

But students do *not* really need most of the terms described in traditional school grammars—or in this book! Using the language more effectively as writers is possible without them: Student writers don't have to remember grammatical terms to comprehend, appreciate, and imitate effective examples of language use.

Nevertheless, it does seem important that *teachers* of writing should consciously understand the most basic functions of words and groups of words within sentences, the different kinds of modifying constructions that they can teach to students, and the conventions of standard edited American English. Ideally, teachers will even be able to analyze key aspects of sentences, so that they can select good examples from literature and from their own students' writing and not be powerlessly tied to prepackaged curriculums.

Practical, productive grammar is eclectic, drawing on more than one approach to describing language and its use. Traditional schoolroom grammar is fraught with contradictions and unnecessary distinctions. The grammatical descriptions here and in the following chapters are something of a hybrid. I've drawn upon traditional terms when they aren't likely to confuse and/or when they are so common that many teachers would be lost without them. But the grammatical descriptions here are not simply my version of a traditional grammar text. To construct a grammar that's useful for teachers of writing, we also need to draw on grammatical descriptions and explanations provided by *linguists,* who study language and try to describe or explain it accurately. The aim is to provide teachers with what they most need to help students enrich and enhance their writing and be able to answer many of their students' questions about the language.

> *Student writers don't have to remember grammatical terms to comprehend, appreciate, and imitate effective examples of language use.*

Linguistic grammars

Those familiar with linguistic analyses of language will recognize that the treatment of grammar in this book sometimes draws upon insights from *transformational* grammar, developed initially by linguist Noam Chomsky in *Syntactic Structures* (1957) and *Aspects of the Theory of Syntax* (1965); the *structural* analyses of grammar as presented earlier by linguists Charles C. Fries (1952), Paul Roberts (1956), and W. N. Francis (1958); the *functional* grammars of linguists like M. A. K. Halliday (1985) and his successors, such as John Collerson (1994) and Norman Fairclough (1989); and the current work of linguists like Martha Kolln and Robert Funk in *Understanding English Grammar* (2006). Unfortunately, none of the linguistic traditions have really caught on in U.S. schools, despite their insights, but such linguists' work has influenced the grammatical descriptions many of us use in writing for teachers and students today.

Background concepts

Basic parts of speech

1. A *noun* designates someone or something: *girl, puppy, flower, money, idea, love*. Any word or group of words that works like a single noun is a *nominal*.

2. A *pronoun* can "take the place of" or "stand for" a noun (or noun phrase): *he, me, your, his, this, that, which, who, someone, anything, nobody*, etc. Therefore a pronoun is also a nominal. (Nominals have several basic functions, which will be discussed in other chapters as needed.)

3. A *verb* expresses action or state of being. For example, a verb tells what a subject noun does, is doing, or did: *he <u>skis</u>, he <u>is skiing</u>, he <u>skied</u>*. When two or more words work together as a verb, they are usually called a *verb phrase*, as in <u>is skiing</u>. (It would be more logical to call such a phrase a "verbal," but that's not traditional.) Here are the forms of the verb *to be*: *am, is, are, was, were, be, being, been*. This is the major, though not the only, verb that expresses a state of being.

4. An *adjective* is a word that modifies a noun. Any word or group of words working like a single adjective is an *adjectival*.

   That was a <u>corny</u> joke.

   Herb wrote some poems <u>about working in a grocery store</u>.

   The excitement <u>that was generated by Superman's appearance</u> couldn't be quelled.

5. An *adverb* is a word that modifies a verb. Any word or group of words working like a single adverb is an *adverbial*. Sometimes an adverbial seems to modify the whole action specified in a sentence. Adverbials usually tell in what manner (how), to what extent (how long, how far, and so on), where, when, or why with respect to the action.

   <u>Ironically</u>, I've been getting stressed <u>while editing materials on stress reduction</u>.

   <u>With a steady hand</u>, Kim retraced the drawing <u>in darker ink</u>.

   Mark <u>quickly</u> zoomed <u>into the one empty parking space</u>.

   We waited <u>twenty-four hours</u>.

   <u>Then</u> we called the police, <u>because we didn't know what else to do</u>.

6. A *preposition* is a word like *in, on, by, to*, or *around* when it introduces a noun, pronoun, or noun phrase (nominal). Examples: *<u>in</u> the box, <u>on</u> it, <u>by</u> the brightly colored box, <u>to</u> the big box, <u>around</u> the mysterious box*. Together, the preposition + the following nominal constitute a *prepositional phrase*.

7. A *coordinating conjunction* joins two grammatical elements of the same kind. *And* and *but* are the most common, followed by *or, so,* and *yet.* Other words that sometimes conjoin two sentences are *for* and *nor,* and the pairs *either . . . or, neither . . . nor.* (Some people have learned an acronym for remembering the basic coordinating conjunctions: FANBOYS, which stands for *for, and, nor, but, or, yet, so.*)

8. *Subordinating conjunctions* are words that begin adverb clauses. Or to put it another way, when we place a subordinating conjunction in front of a sentence, we have made it into a subordinate clause: a piece of a sentence. Example: <u>*When*</u> *you're through,* put your materials away; I had to quit, <u>*though*</u> *I wasn't finished yet.* (See the explanation that follows under "Clauses and Phrases.")

Basic parts of a sentence: subject + predicate

1. The verb is crucial to a sentence. (See the preceding definition of verbs.) The verb or verb phrase can stand alone as a *predicate,* but many verbs require something to follow them: *I petted* <u>*the dog*</u> (direct object); *Marvin was* <u>*my first dog*</u> (predicate nominal); *my dog was* <u>*very rambunctious*</u> (predicate adjectival).

2. The *subject* usually (but not always) specifies who or what is doing the action or is in the state specified by the verb. The subject may be any word or group of words that can work as a noun: a nominal, in other words. Here are some basic two-word sentences, subject plus verb:

Computers quit.	Hope endures.	Zack left.	Malcolm grinned.
They laughed.	She smirked.	Nobody cried.	Everyone smiled.

Clauses and phrases

1. A *clause* contains a subject plus a complete verb unit. In the following example, *being* is not a complete verb: *Jack* <u>*being*</u> *ready now.*

   a. A clause that can stand alone as a grammatically complete sentence is an *independent (main) clause.* (A sentence that has only one clause, an independent clause, is called a *simple sentence.* A sentence with two or more independent clauses is a *compound sentence.*)

   b. A clause that is grammatically tied to, or part of, another clause is a *subordinate clause.*

For example:

I can't wait <u>until you are ready to leave.</u>

<u>Although the champ was stronger,</u> his opponent was more clever.

This is the one that I wanted.

That was his secret, which he finally told me.

I know what you mean.

She knew that she shouldn't do it.

She knew it was wrong.

A *complex sentence* contains one independent clause and at least one subordinate clause.

2. A *phrase* is a group of words that functions together as a unit but does not contain a subject plus a complete verb. In this example, the underlined phrase modifies *plane*: *The plane taxiing down the runway was designed by Peter's father.* Many modifiers are phrases.

Don't worry if you haven't fully grasped these concepts yet: You can come back to the definitions as needed. Most important, though, you can still understand the functions of modifiers! Don't get lost in the "trees" of these definitions; aim instead for the "forest" of making sentences more informative and interesting through modifiers.

Don't get lost in the "trees" of these definitions; aim instead for the "forest" of making sentences more informative and interesting through modifiers.

What are modifiers, and why teach them?

A *modifier* is simply a grammatical construction that describes, specifies, adjusts—or *modifies*—something in a sentence. A modifier can be a word, a phrase, or a clause. But most important is what a modifier does: It adds detail to a bare-bones sentence.

Bound and free modifiers

A *bound* adjectival modifier is one that is supposedly needed to clarify who or what is being talked about.

A *free* adjectival modifier gives additional information about an entity: information that is interesting or useful, but not essential to clarifying who or what. A free modifier is "set off" by commas. This means that if the free modifier begins the sentence, it has a comma after it; if it comes somewhere in the middle of the sentence, it has a comma before and after it; if it comes at the end of the sentence, it has a comma before it.

Adverbial modifiers are "free" if they are movable within a sentence. Comma use with free adverbial modifiers varies, depending on the nature of the adverbial and its location.

Free modifiers are easy to teach, easy to learn and use, and make a substantial difference in the quality and sophistication of students' writing. In this book, I focus on modifiers in narrative/descriptive writing as a foundation for learning to add detail in all genres of writing.

Modifiers are either adjectival or adverbial, by definition. Which constructions should we teach? The ones that seem to need most instructional coaxing are adjectival: *appositives*, *participial phrases*, and *absolutes* (Christensen & Christensen, 1978). To these may be added "adjectives out of order," as Harry Noden calls them (1999, p. 9), a category that I have expanded in this chapter. These are all what Christensen called "free modifiers": free in that (1) they are set off from the rest of the sentence by a comma (or two commas) and (2) they can often be moved to at least one other position in a sentence.

Judicious use of these constructions goes a long way in producing writing that sounds, grammatically, more like the writing of professionals. Such constructions, among others, constitute the "tighter coiling of thought" that Walter Loban (1976) noticed decades ago among more competent and older student writers.

The following sections describe the four kinds of adjectival phrases that most need to be taught, followed by the adverbial clause, which is also especially worth teaching. Chapter 4 will illustrate such teaching with two of these four kinds of adjectival phrases. These are all free modifying constructions.

In the following sections, simplistic examples are abandoned in favor of richer examples from a work of literature, the junior novel *Circle of Magic: Sandry's Book* (1997), by Tamora Pierce. In this beautifully written fantasy, the unusual abilities of four ten- to twelve-year-olds are discovered, nurtured, and employed in saving themselves and others. The four children are named Sandry, Trisana (Tris), Briar, and Daja.

Importance of modifiers

Explaining the importance of teaching modifiers, Francis Christensen (1967) quotes John Erskine (1946):

> When you write, you make a point, not by subtracting as though you sharpened a pencil, but by adding. When you put one word after another, your statement should be more precise the more you add. . . . What you wish to say is found not in the noun but in what you add to qualify the noun. The noun is only a grappling iron to hitch your mind to the reader's. . . . The noun, the verb, and the main clause serve merely as a base on which the meaning will rise.
>
> The modifier is the essential part of any sentence. (cited in Christensen, pp. 24–25)

Adjectivals

As explained, modifying words and phrases are called *adjectival* ("working like an adjective") when they modify a noun (or pronoun). The four kinds of free modifying adjectivals, as categorized here, are the *appositive*, *"out-of-order" adjectivals*, *present participials*, and the *absolute* construction. As we shall see, free adjectival modifiers may occur at the beginning of a sentence or clause, where they look ahead to the subject; right after the noun they modify; or later in the sentence, when it is clear what they modify.

Appositives

An appositive is a noun—or a nominal with a primary ("head") noun or pronoun—that most commonly comes right after another noun that it describes. The appositive may serve as a near-synonym for the noun, renaming it in a different way. In many instances the appositive specifies a category into which the modified noun fits. Sometimes it simply elaborates on the modified noun. In every case, an appositive is set off by a comma or commas from the rest of the sentence (or occasionally by dashes or a colon). An appositive is a noun or nominal in form, but it functions adjectivally, to clarify the nature of another noun/nominal:

> The metal-and-enamel image of Yalina, <u>goddess of water</u>, dropped from the shelf on which it sat. (p. 42)

> <u>A city girl</u>, she had always known that the air she felt, even on rooftops, had its teeth drawn as it passed over encircling walls to pick up all the smells of busy humans, not land, sea, or rock. (p. 61)

As the last example indicates, occasionally an appositive modifies a pronoun.

The following examples are based on but not directly taken from *Sandry's Book*:

> Tris grumpily thrust the thread at Sandry, <u>an adept weaver of cloth</u>.

> The miniature tree, <u>a stubborn critter if Briar ever saw one</u>, simply refused to die.

Appositives are free modifiers, and they can occur not only right after the noun they clarify, but before it:

> <u>A stubborn critter if Briar ever saw one</u>, the miniature tree simply refused to die.

> Briar, <u>an unlikely apprentice if there ever was one</u>, finally learned his craft.

> <u>An unlikely apprentice if there ever was one</u>, Briar finally learned his craft.

> <u>A natural as a metalworker</u>, Daja could handle red-hot iron.

> Daja, <u>a natural as a metalworker</u>, could handle red-hot iron.

"Out-of-order" adjectivals

Harry Noden, in *Image Grammar* (1999), has characterized as "adjectives out of order" those adjectives that occur at the beginning of a sentence; right *after* the noun they modify; or at the end of the sentence (even if they modify the subject). Such adjectives—singly, in pairs, or in threes—are set off from the rest of the sentence by a comma or commas. The first four examples come from *Sandry's Book*:

> <u>Bare</u>, it looked like a child's top with much too long a stem. (p. 94)

> <u>Nervous</u> and <u>eager</u>, Sandry obeyed. (p. 96)

> She stared up at him, <u>terrified</u>. (p. 131)

Stocky, broad-shouldered, and commanding, the duke preferred simple clothes. (p. 23)

Daja, angry and hurt, stomped out of the forge.

Angry and hurt, Daja stomped out of the forge.

Daja stomped out of the forge, angry and hurt.

Sandry, oblivious, focused on the cloth she was making for bandages.

Oblivious, Sandry focused on the cloth she was making for bandages.

Gratified, Tris ventured a slow smile.

Tris, gratified, ventured a slow smile.

Perhaps more often, an adjectivally headed phrase—not just one adjective or a set of them—will occur right after the noun modified or at the beginning or end of the sentence. Here are some actual sentences from *Sandry's Book* and a few more based on the book:

About to touch him, she changed her mind. (p. 31)

Alone on deck, she heard thunder growl in the distance. (p. 34)

Storm clouds rolled by, heavy with rain and thunder. (p. 50)

Sandry toyed with her fork, bored almost to tears. (p. 37)

Angry and hurt by his accusation, Daja stomped out of the forge.

Sandry, oblivious to their wide-eyed stares, focused on the cloth she was making for bandages.

Beside her they placed her few bags, completely packed. (p. 18)

Gratified by her mentor's praise, Tris ventured a slow smile.

Rung only for emergencies, the bell pealed now over their threatened land.

Which of the preceding modifiers can be moved to at least one other place in the sentence? Would any or all of these modifiers sound as good somewhere else in the sentence?

Teachers with a background in traditional grammar may notice that the head of each phrase in the last three sentences is a past participle. A *past participle* is the form of a verb that would follow *have, has, had*, or *having*, as in: *They had rung the bell only twice before*, or *Niko's praise has gratified Tris beyond measure*. It seemed most sensible to include such phrases within this adjectival phrase category rather than to create a separate category for them.

Present participials

Present participles and especially participial phrases, on the other hand, occur so frequently in published writing that they deserve a category of their own and separate lessons for teaching them. (See Chapter 2 for an extended example of teaching participial phrases in the context of writing.)

A *present participle* is what the *-ing* form of a verb is called when it functions adjectivally, to modify a noun. Our concern here is with modifiers that are not closely bound to their noun:

> <u>Whistling</u>, Briar took it and walked right into a shaft of light that nearly blinded him. (p. 90)

> <u>Blinking</u>, he shielded his eyes to find its source. (p. 90)

Most often a present participial modifier is a phrase rather than a single word:

> <u>Darting over to the rail</u>, she turned up her face just as a tall wave slapped the ship. (p. 34)

> A globe of fire leaped to another mast, <u>clinging to its top</u>. (p. 35)

> Power rolled away from her, <u>growing to include the others, spreading around the hollow, taking the shape that meant safety to Daja</u> Kisubo. (p. 230)

> Through and around her braid, light shone steadily, <u>filling the room with a soft, pearly glow</u>. (p. 59)

Interestingly, most of these *-ing* phrases cannot be sensibly moved elsewhere in the sentence unless the sentence is changed just a little. They are technically "free" modifiers because they are set off by commas, but in these contexts, most are not freely movable.

Most of the time, though, a present participial phrase can be moved from one position in the sentence to at least one other. (See examples in Part 2, Section A.)

Absolutes

An absolute is almost a sentence, but not quite. Typically it is lacking only *was* or *were* to be a complete sentence. In other words, most absolutes could be restored to a full sentence by adding *was* or *were*. Sometimes the absolute refers back, grammatically, to something in the main clause:

> Daja watched him go, <u>her hand tightening on her staff until her knuckles were white</u>. (p. 185)

> The Trader was glaring at everyone, <u>her chin up</u>, <u>the dark skin of her cheeks burning red</u>. (p. 38)

Little Bear, his belly round with the meal of scraps he had gulped, sprawled on the floor and slept, paws twitching as he dreamed. (p. 201)

Briar, his range much broader now, reached to the earth's surface. (p. 240)

The room was plain and clean, its walls covered with a coat of whitewash. (p. 201)

An absolute acts like a zoom lens, zooming in to focus on a detail of someone or something. While some absolutes do contain participial phrases, these participials are not set off as separate "free" modifiers; the participial phrases are part of the total absolute.

Notice that each set-off absolute could be restored to a full sentence with the addition of *was* or *were*. But since the absolute is not grammatically complete, it cannot stand alone as a sentence.

Sometimes an absolute has no grammatical relationship at all with the main clause:

She stood alone on deck, the low-slung moon casting a path across the water.

The weather finally improved, Briar was able to plant his herbs.

Notice that the last sentence is not a comma splice sentence, with two independent clauses separated by just a comma. The first clause, *the weather finally improved*, sets the scene for what Briar is doing. One way we can tell this seeming clause is actually an absolute is to put *with* in front of it: *With the weather finally improved, Briar was able to plant his herbs*. The sentence sounds good—perhaps even better—that way. Francis Christensen, who revived the concept of the absolute, suggests that even if we put *with* at the beginning of an absolute, it can still be considered an absolute, not a prepositional phrase (Christensen & Christensen, 1978).

Another example of an absolute not related grammatically to anything else comes from *The Waterless Sea*, by Kate Constable (2003, p. 63): *The space in which they crouched was untouched by the storm, the sand beneath them a smooth circle of calm*. The absolutes that have no grammatical relationship with the main sentence may seem to have an adverbial sense, describing the scene rather than a person or thing.

Adjectival phrases: Bringing them all together

There are many ways to bring the different kinds of adjectival phrases together, particularly the kinds that most need modeling and teaching. One simple way, however, is to write and share "I am" poems as models. An "I

From grammar to rhetoric

When we begin to consider which options are best, we are slipping from grammar into rhetoric, which deals with making effective choices in a given context. As Francis Christensen wrote in *Notes Toward a New Rhetoric* (1967, p. 39), "Grammar maps out the possible; rhetoric narrows the possible down to the desirable or effective." Good teaching of writing encompasses both.

am" poem metaphorically equates the writer with things that typify his or her life, interests, hopes, or fantasies. Here is an example I wrote:

I am
A faded pair of bluejeans,
    caressing hips and thighs,
A box of cheese crackers,
    salty, crunchy, fattening,
A bargain basement shopper,
    my arms laden with clothes marked 70 percent off—
A cozy, comfy blanket,
    winter's substitute for love.

This poem illustrates a present participial phrase ("caressing hips and thighs"), adjectives after a noun ("salty, crunchy, fattening"), an absolute ("my arms laden with clothes marked 70 percent off"), and an appositive ("winter's substitute for love"). The poem was fun to write, too! I invite you to create similar models and, after teaching these four constructions, to share the models as invitations to students to include all four in their own "I am" poem.

Adverbial clauses

In general, a *subordinate clause* is a subject-verb unit that cannot stand alone as a grammatically complete sentence, though occasionally one may be written that way for effect.

A *subordinate adverbial clause* is one that functions like an adverb. Subordinated to a main clause, the adverbial clause "modifies" the main clause. In particular, a subordinate clause that indicates time or sequence, cause, condition, or concession is typically an *adverbial clause* modifying the entire main clause. Such clauses are introduced by subordinating conjunctions like *after, before, since, until; because, so that; if, unless, whether;* and *although, though, even though.* Here are some examples from *Sandry's Book*:

Sandry dug in her belt-purse <u>until she found a small glass vial with a silver filigree cap.</u> (p. 112)

<u>When the fumes from the smelling salts burned her nose,</u> she gasped and sneezed. (p. 112)

<u>As the staircase door closed behind them,</u> all four halted and looked around. (p. 113)

<u>If the man hadn't turned away,</u> the flying end might have lashed his face. (p. 134)

Carrying the wire out of the cubicle, he put it on an anvil and turned it several times, <u>as if he turned sausages in a frying pan.</u> (p. 135)

Teaching subordinate adverbial clauses

This lesson, focusing on adverbial clauses and the subordinators that introduce them, is suitable for middle school on up. I begin by reading aloud Cynthia Rylant's picture book *When I Was Young in the Mountains* (1982), a personal favorite of mine. Then I share a related poem that I wrote to model how we could all write such poems based on our own lives. Having deliberately included some details I thought students would find humorous, I share the following poem orally, put it on the overhead, and discuss key features with the class.

When I Was Young in the Country

Connie Weaver

When I was young in the country,
    we lived in a red brick house
    perched atop a hill.
    The house stood like a sentinel
    surveying the countryside,
    its dormer windows shining with light.

When I was young in the country,
    my big brother used to babysit me,
    rocking my cradle with one foot,
    holding a rifle in his arms to protect us.
    The nighttime noises of crickets and tree toads
    scared him.

When I was young in the country,
    I refused to eat cottage cheese and tomatoes,
    an affront to my delicate tastebuds.
    After dinner, I sampled them from the dog's dish.

When I was young in the country,
    my dog Daisy often chased me,
    grasping at my diapers and
    pulling them down.
    I was too little to be embarrassed.

I loved growing up in the country.

You may have noticed that I used an appositive, an absolute, several present participial phrases, and a bound postnoun adjectival ("perched atop a hill"). I might point out the *-ing* phrases to students, but otherwise I simply leave the other constructions to stand as models, if desired.

Next, I invite students to at least begin their own "When I was . . ." poem. Unfortunately, though, I haven't saved any student examples to share. Teachers may need to give students help, particularly in sequencing their sentences or stanzas and in adding the comma after the introductory subordinate clause.

There are many ways to follow up, such as asking students to write other sentences of their choice, with different subordinators. It may be worthwhile to consider whether or not these adverbial clauses sound good in more than one location in the sentence. (A comma is optional before a subordinate clause that ends the sentence.) Another picture book that can stimulate such writing is *If You're Not from the Prairie . . .* by David Bouchard (1993). Obviously these books also contain excellent examples for teaching parallel constructions. Teachers may want to have students write their own poems, their own picture books, or a class picture book using a particular subordinator. For students who are writing persuasive and argumentative pieces, it may be especially appropriate to create a class or individual picture book on a particular topic, beginning their sentences with *although*, *even though*, or another subordinator showing contrast.

Here's a list of common subordinating conjunctions (some have other uses, too):

Time: after, as, as soon as, before, since, till, until, when, while
Cause: as, because, in order that, since, so that
Condition: as if, assuming that, if, in case, unless, when, whether
Contrast: although, even though, rather than, though, whereas, while

Learning to use these subordinators in creative contexts can go a long way toward making sentences flow logically in explanatory and persuasive prose.

How to Launch the Teaching of Modifiers

Is there a one-size-fits-all recipe for teaching modifiers to your students? Of course not—unless you choose to teach directly from one of the sentence-combining books described at the end of Chapter 1. Harry Noden's forthcoming *Image Grammar Activities Book* will be an excellent resource as well. But my advice is simply to start experimenting. Take risks! As any teacher knows, what works well with one class may not work well with another, so we have to keep trying new things to learn what works in our own classrooms. Gradually our own concept of "best practice" will emerge as we find strategies and procedures that work more often than not.

You need not be alone in your experimentation, however. Talk to and work with other teachers. Share your lesson ideas, get feedback, help your teacher mates, and together compile sets of materials and ideas that have worked for you. This chapter is meant to encourage and assist you, not only by offering general guidelines and advice but also by describing some of my own experiments in teaching free modifying adjectivals. Some of these experiments have been a grand success, others a partial success, but all have been enjoyable, because I haven't been uptight about taking risks. Therefore, my experiments have all been wonderful learning experiences as well.

Where and how to begin?

By "where" to begin, I mean with what grammatical construction or constructions. Of the four discussed in detail in the previous chapter, the easiest to teach and the easiest for students to learn seem to be out-of-order adjectives and the participial phrase. I haven't taught out-of-order adjectives below the middle grades, but I suspect it can be done successfully by providing models and teaching the revision strategy of taking a prenoun adjective and moving it to a postnoun position, with a comma or commas to set it off. As for present participial phrases, I know that these *-ing* phrases can be taught successfully as early as first grade!

This chapter illustrates the teaching of two free modifying constructions: the present participial phrase and the absolute. Participial phrases are easy to teach and they occur frequently in all genres: description and narration, poetry, biography and autobiography, informative and persuasive prose, and (a relatively new genre) creative nonfiction. I illustrate just the narrative/descriptive genre here, not only to keep things simple and manageable but also because I believe that learning to use modifiers in that genre lays the groundwork for using details—not just modifiers, but information—in informative and persuasive prose. Absolutes, on the other hand, seem to be the most difficult for teachers to understand, let alone teach, but they are well worth including in a writer's repertoire. As my son said at age fifteen, when I asked how he'd learned to use the absolutes in one of his poems, "Oh, all writers know how to use those."

So how to begin? First, we will revisit the general framework from Chapter 2 (see the adjacent box) for teaching important grammatical constructions; you might also reconsider the teaching examples in Chapter 2. We may all deviate from this model in practice, but it's a good reminder of a structure that typically works well. To begin, focus on just the first four steps. Some classes will require only a couple of the steps, while other classes—and more challenging grammatical concepts—will require more examples and additional teacher guidance before most students can create their own sentences successfully.

In teaching modifying constructions, I draw on several techniques:

Idealized framework for teaching grammatical concepts

1. Share a model
   - from literature
   - from a previous or current student
   - created by the teacher in advance
   - composed by the teacher on the spot

2. Create another model
   - teacher
   - teacher and students together

3. Compose (or do a related activity) in small groups or pairs; share and clarify as needed.

4. Compose a sentence or sentences individually; share. Teacher can check the work if desired and possible.

---

1. *Sentence imitating.* I share one or more model sentences, discuss the grammar of the modifier with the students, and ask them (in groups, pairs, or individually) to create their own sentence or sentences following the pattern used in the model. This is generally easy for students to do; it's also highly motivating, because they are creating their own sentences, not combining someone else's.

2. *Sentence expanding.* After sharing and discussing model sentences, I ask students to expand a sentence with a modifier that follows the pattern used in the model. The basic sentence may be one I suggest, one we have brainstormed as a class, or one the student has written.

3. *Sentence combining.* This requires the least independent thought and creativity on the part of the students and is therefore likely to be the least motivating. However, I sometimes use this technique in preparation for sentence expanding or sentence imitating, especially when we are working as a class. I have also used this technique with teachers—not only to demonstrate the technique but also to suggest how they

can help students combine their own sentences when they revise their writing.

The ultimate goal is for students to use these constructions not only independently but automatically in their own writing.

Introducing participial phrases

Present participial phrases effectively subordinate a detail to a main statement or describe a process. They keep you from having to resort to sentences of the same basic structure that go *clunk, clunk, clunk* across the page. But how to teach the use of such modifiers?

My first experience doing so was spontaneous. My college freshmen had been writing "I am" poems (there's an example toward the end of Chapter 3), some of which included present participial phrases: noun modifiers headed by the *-ing* form of a verb. I had not taught *or* modeled that construction; the students simply used the *–ing* phrases naturally. After the first teacher in-service I ever offered on teaching writing, since I was now considered a "grammar expert," I was invited to visit a college teacher's "remedial" writing class, in which the students' daily work consisted of completing exercises in a grammar workbook (complete with answers at the back). But as we walked down the corridor to the classroom, the teacher seemed nervous about being observed and suggested that, instead, I talk to the class about how I approached teaching grammar. Oh, great, I thought; this will never do. Then unexpectedly, I found myself offering, "Would you like me to teach the class?" I was remembering my students' "I am" poems, thinking about their participial phrases, and optimistically figuring I could somehow teach these to the students.

I had no models, no lesson plans, and—until inspiration hit—not even a concrete idea for how to teach this construction, since my own students had begun using it spontaneously. But as I entered the classroom, I knew I wanted to have these students write "I am" poems using *-ing* phrases, and I hit upon the idea of having the students metaphorically equate themselves with a piece of sports equipment: *I am a canoe,* for example, or *I am a baseball bat,* or *I am a football*—whatever caught their fancy.

I had the class brainstorm pieces of sports equipment, then choose one item to write about as a whole class. The Frisbee was a popular choice, so I had students brainstorm a couple of prenoun adjectives. Their choices were "red" and "square" (of all things!), so I wrote on the board "I am a red, square Frisbee." (We discussed which adjective should go first, and they decided.) "Okay," I said, "What might the Frisbee be doing?" "It might crash through a window," someone said. "A canine's jaws," someone else said; "it could land in the grip of a canine's jaws." Wow! "Sailing through the air," another student said. "A Frisbee sails through the air."

Intent on a sentence-combining approach to our task, I wrote the students' ideas in uniformly structured sentences under our main sentence:

I am a red, square Frisbee.

The Frisbee is crashing through a window.

The Frisbee is landing in the grip of a canine's jaws.

The Frisbee is sailing through the air.

As you can see from the awkward sentence about the canine's jaws, I was fixated on my plan to write sentences that could be reduced to participial phrases! It was easy to cross out "The Frisbee is" from each sentence, have the students tell me in what order the details should logically occur, and thereby produce our model, complete with the needed commas:

I am a square, red Frisbee,

sailing through the air,

crashing through a window,

and landing in the grip of a canine's jaws.

The next step was to invite the students to choose their own piece of sports equipment—it could be from the class list but didn't have to be— and write their own participle poem. (I used the term *present participle phrase* initially, since these were older students, but then reverted to the simpler *-ing phrase*.)

Toward the end of the class, I asked for volunteers to share their "I am" poems. I especially remember one that started "I am a young lawn-mower," followed by seven or eight participial phrases. The lesson had been highly successful!

As the teacher and I walked back down the corridor from her class-room, she remarked, almost in awe: "I never knew they could write like that!" Of course not: The prescribed course of study had them doing grammar exercises instead of using grammatical resources in their own writing.

To review, let's go back to the general framework for teaching a grammatical concept over time. In this spontaneous teaching situation, composing a model together was a collapsing of steps 1 and 2 on sharing and composing models. Then we leaped over step 3, composing in smaller groups or pairs, and went straight to step 4, composing individually. This demonstrates what I mean by the framework being "general": a list of steps from which we can draw as appropriate or possible, not a Procrustean bed into which we all must fit.

Since that time, I have discovered that it is easy for students to add *-ing* phrases to a base sentence without first reducing or otherwise changing complete sentences to *-ing* phrases. Not long ago, a class of fourth graders at the Greenwich (Connecticut) Country Day School proved this to me beyond any doubt. True, the school is private and exclusive, but clearly it was the excellent writing workshop approach of their teacher, Sarah Cauldwell, that made the greatest difference in what the students could do: From the very outset, they seemed to be more eager if not also more capable writers than significantly older students in the same school system who were studying grammar instead of writing. At any rate, most of my preparation was unnecessary!

I had decided to work with the "I am" poem again, but to have the students write "I am" poems about animals. First, I put my own starter sentence on the smart board: "I am a frisky squirrel." I told the class I had written a poem about what the squirrel was doing, such as hiding nuts, and immediately they began to offer other *-ing* phrases to describe what a squirrel does. The class had been working on using strong verbs, and it showed: They produced interesting *-ing* words to head their phrases, offered phrases faster than I could write them, and were still offering more when I had run out of room on the smart board.

Quickly, then, we brainstormed a list of animals, both domestic and wild—"zoo" animals, they said. Most students were quick to choose an animal to write about and had at least some *-ing* phrases before the forty-five-minute class period ended. The only problem arose with children who had chosen a wild animal they really didn't know much about.

The teacher followed up on my lesson, and the following week the students created a book of their own "I am" animal poems with beautiful animal illustrations. (See the examples in Figure 4–1; however, these retyped versions do not include the images and don't do justice to the children's creative use of type fonts and colors.) Clearly the students had help in developing their ideas, not only in the classroom but possibly at home: The poems are more like—or better than—what one might ordinarily get from high school writers, even if they too had received assistance. The fourth graders' poems show what can be accomplished, with guidance, in literacy-rich classrooms.

I often use literary models in teaching present participial phrases. Deciding to use literary sentences as models for a fifth-grade class studying the American Revolution, I chose (and sometimes simplified) some sentences from Avi's *The Fighting Ground* (1984), which some of these fifth graders were reading. Whenever possible, I recommend choosing examples from literature (including nonfiction) that students have already read, are currently reading, or are about to read in class—or that you think they might be interested in reading.

A related activity that students often enjoy is for the teacher to take a passage from a literary work, simplify the sentences, and—without showing the original to the students—invite them to combine some of the sentences to make the paragraph flow better. Comparing their versions with the original often triggers important insights into writing styles and options.

Oddly enough, it is teachers themselves with whom I have most often used sentence combining as a strategy for producing present participial phrases. Why? Partly, I think, just because I used to be enamored of

Horse

I am a horse,
    Rearing at the horse show,
    Bucking off my rider,
    Trotting calmly in the ring,
    Grazing in the grass while the winds
are blowing swiftly.
        —Alie

Fox

I am a fox,
    Slipping slyly through the trees,
    Chasing chickens and eating them,
    Quietly searching through the snow,
    Leaping over fallen trees,
    Running happily on the field,
    Taking care of my young,
    Alert of any danger.
        —Leigh

Mouse

I am a mouse
    Scampering around for food
    Sneaking through the house
    Dodging slickly left and right
    Running into a human
    Slipping away sneakily.
        —Jonathan

Jaguar

I am a jaguar,
    pouncing on my prey,
    tearing animals in two,
    bounding through the forest,
    cleaning my silky coat,
    taking care of my young,
    and doing my duty as a jaguar.
        —Dana

Dragon

I am a dragon
    sending helpless knights up in flames
        when leaving my cavern
    searching for hidden treasures
    devouring sheep and cows, yum!
    burning flames shoot out of my mouth
    destroying towns, cities and people
    attacking other dragons for their treasures
    going to my cavern only to find a heroic
        knight sent to slay me
    falling down with a cut
    blood over my treasures
    full stomach
    feeling poisoned
    falling asleep on top of my piles
        of treasures
    possibly to never wake again.
        —William Sternlicht

Puppy

I am a puppy,
    Jumping through the air,
    Pouncing in the leaves,
    Shivering with delight,
    Jumping after the frightened Frisbee
    Getting the Frisbee with glee.
        —Lila

Dolphin

I am a Dolphin
    sliding through the waves
    laughing at a flashy fish

    leaping over the foam topped waves,
    feeling the fading sun on my back,
    watching the stars from under the sea

    Closing my eyes and letting sleep
        envelope me
        —Claire Shope

FIGURE 4–1 Animal poems from Sarah Cauldwell's fourth-grade class

sentence combining, considering it *the* way to teach any and all of the free modifying constructions. But partly, too, I have teachers try sentence combining to demonstrate how they can draw two or more sentences from a student's writing that would be more effective combined than separate and, with the student's permission, use the sentences to teach a minilesson on combining sentences.

If you create, for your own students, some sentence-combining activities designed to produce present participial phrases, keep in mind that you do not have to have an *-ing* verb in the sentence that will become the participial phrase. Sentences with past tense verbs are more likely what you'll find to work with, particularly in student writing. For example, you might start with two sentences like these: *I watched William in the 100-yard relay. He ran faster than any other member of his team.* Although the second sentence does not have an *-ing* verb, you can show students how to create a present participial phrase from it, like this: *I watched William in the 100-yard relay, running faster than any of his teammates.*

Introducing absolutes

When I read about absolute constructions in Francis Christensen's *Notes Toward a New Rhetoric* (1967), I was intrigued that almost any sentence containing a present or past tense form of *to be* (*is*, *are*, *was*, or *were* but rarely *am*) can be made into an absolute construction simply by deleting the form of *be*. Here are some recent examples from two Harry Potter books by J. K. Rowling.

From *Harry Pottter and the Goblet of Fire* (2000):

> It stood on a hill overlooking the village, <u>some of its windows boarded</u>, <u>tiles missing from its roof</u>, and <u>ivy spreading unchecked over its face</u>. (p. 1)

> <u>The letter finished</u>, he tied it to Hedwig's leg . . . . (p. 37)

> Fred and George were sitting in a far corner, <u>quills out</u>, talking in whispers, <u>their heads bent over a piece of parchment</u>. (p. 152)

> Next to it, and in the very center of the table, sat Professor Dumbledore, the headmaster, <u>his sweeping silver hair and beard shining in the candlelight</u>, <u>his magnificent deep green robes embroidered with many stars and moons</u>. (p. 175)

From *Harry Potter and the Half-Blood Prince* (2005):

> A grandfather clock lay splintered at their feet, <u>its face cracked</u>, <u>its pendulum lying a little farther away like a dropped sword</u>. (p. 63)

> Harry nodded, <u>his mouth so full of hot soup that he could not speak</u>. (p. 83)

Eyes still watering and head still throbbing, he [Harry] drew his wand, careful not to disarrange the cloak, and waited, breath held. (p. 153)

"The very best of evenings to you!" he [Dumbledore] said, smiling broadly, his arms opened wide as though to embrace the whole room. (p. 165)

Each of these absolutes can be restored to a full sentence by adding *was* or *were*, as appropriate, though with *breath held*, we also have to add *Harry's* or *his*. Thus we can say that a sentence with *was* or *were* (or *is*, *are*, and theoretically *am*) can be made into an absolute by eliminating its specific form of *to be*. Let's recreate one of those sentences by deconstructing and then reconstructing a sentence from *Harry Potter and the Goblet of Fire*. Here's the original sentence:

It stood on a hill overlooking the village, some of its windows boarded, tiles missing from its roof, and ivy spreading unchecked over its face. (p. 1)

Deconstructing each of the absolutes, we get:

It stood on a hill overlooking the village. Some of its windows were boarded. Tiles were missing from its roof. Ivy was spreading unchecked over its face.

Deleting *were* and *was* from these "underlying" sentences, all we have to do is fix the punctuation and capitalization and add *and* in order to return to the original sentence: *It stood on a hill overlooking the village, some of its windows boarded, tiles missing from its roof, and ivy spreading unchecked over its face.* Sometimes sentences deconstructed like this can be recombined in more than one way, giving students more authority over the sentence combining.

I developed the sentence-combining activity in Figure 4–2 using examples from Robert Ludlum's *The Sigma Protocol* (2001), which I was reading at the time. I created simple sentences from several of Ludlum's original constructions, so that when the *was* or w*ere* was deleted from the second sentence in each set (and in one case, the third as well), the result would be an absolute. Alternatively, literary models can simply be imitated.

Recently I have taught absolutes in two subcategories: those that give *action* details, and those that give *descriptive* details. (I haven't yet included the ones that bear no grammatical relationship to the main clause; see the discussion of absolutes in Chapter 2 or in Part 2, Section A4-d, for examples.) The sentences in the examples that follow are taken from or based on Ben Mikaelsen's *Touching Spirit Bear* (2001), a thought-provoking book about an out-of-control fifteen-year-old, Cole Matthews, who is about to be tried as an adult for beating and permanently crippling a

Sentence Combining to Create Absolutes

Make the second (or second and third) sentence in each set into an absolute. Then connect it appropriately to the main sentence.

Example:
She jumped to her feet.   ⟶
Adrenalin ~~was~~ flooding throughout her body.

She jumped to her feet, adrenalin flooding throughout her body.

[However, you can simply mark the changes on the original, underlying sentences.]

1. She jumped to her feet.
   The terror weakened her knees so that she could barely stand up.

2. He slept fitfully.
   His sleep was disturbed by unceasing nightmares in which he was forced to watch the cabin explode time and again.

3. The Paraguayan detective shrugged.
   His hands were spread.
   His eyes were wide with apparent concern.

4. Jimmy Cavanaugh screamed in pain.
   His cry was high-pitched like an animal's.

5. She jumped to her feet.
   Adrenalin flooded throughout her body. [same as the example, but with a past tense verb]

FIGURE 4–2 Sentence-combining activity derived from sentences in Robert Ludlum's *The Sigma Protocol* (2001)

©2007 by Constance Weaver, from *The Grammar Plan Book* (Heinemann: Portsmouth, NH).

classmate. Cole cynically accepts the proffered alternative of having his fate decided by Native American Circle Justice. Sentenced to spend a year mostly alone on a remote island, Cole learns some important life lessons, but not before he foolishly attacks an albino bear locally thought to be a Spirit Bear. The immediate consequences are disastrous: The bear attacks Cole in return, nearly taking his life.

Absolutes that convey action details:

> Cole reeled from the Spirit Bear's attack, <u>his heart pounding with fear</u>, <u>his arms flailing in a useless attempt at defense</u>, <u>his legs giving way underneath him</u>. (The participial phrases occur within the absolute.)

Absolutes that convey descriptive details:

> The Spirit Bear approached Cole with a slow lazy stride, <u>its head held low</u>. (p. 93)

> The Spirit Bear casually licked up the spit, <u>eyes mild and curious</u>. (simplified from p. 93)

> The Spirit Bear towered over him, <u>its rank breath warm</u>. (p. 67)

Now, what do *you* think: Is it easier to imitate the absolutes or to create them through sentence combining? In *Image Grammar* (1999), Harry Noden teaches absolutes that have *-ing* phrases within them, and he teaches these absolutes through sentence imitation, not sentence combining. You, too, might consider teaching just these "action" absolutes first.

Personally, I think sentence imitation is as good an approach to creating absolutes as sentence combining, or perhaps better (see Williams, 1986). This tentative conclusion stems not only from Noden's success with the imitation approach; not only from my hunch and the informal evidence that imitation may be quicker, more motivating, and perhaps just as easy or easier; but also from the work of one particular seventh grader in a class in which I taught absolutes. I never had the opportunity to ask about his process, but from the way his work was arranged on the page, it looked as if he had first created the "final" sentence, complete with absolutes, then dutifully written under it the main sentence, followed by the underlying sentences in which he had crossed out the *was* or *were*.

Another student, Sara Bakrow, apparently did the same thing, creating her sentence with easy flow but then backtracking to show compliance with directions. Her initial/final sentence was:

> 3-year-old Libby, on her father's shoulders, cheered as the parade marched by, her eyes filled with glee, her gurgling laugh ringing above the heads of the crowd, her tiny feet kicking.

On the other hand, other students in the class followed the sentence-combining approach I had led them through, and this seemed to work for them. Brooke Pinto's process went as follows:

Natalie was so interested in her English class. She opened her eyes widely. She took her pencil out and placed [it] in her fingers. Natalie had no idea that class had ended.

↓

Natalie was so interested in her English class, her eyes wide open, her pencil twisting in her fingers, no idea English class had ended.

With some classes, and with the more difficult absolute constructions, it's better to have two go-rounds with models and to include group or pair work (see steps 1–4 in the general framework) before asking students to write independently.

In your initial lessons, experiment with sentence imitation, sentence expansion, and sentence combining; determine for yourself which technique or combination of techniques works especially well. Then, to really make a difference in students' writing, consider teaching the constructions "an inch wide and a mile deep." Having launched your teaching of a concept, reinforce it as your students revise and edit their work. You might give students a revision/editing checklist that includes the concept taught and/or hold group or individual revision/editing conferences as needed, as suggested in Chapter 2. Then return to these procedures again and again with other writing assignments, perhaps beginning anew by sharing fresh literary models and/or composing together and practicing, or perhaps simply attending again to a concept as students revise and edit—whatever degree of reteaching is needed. The steps for teaching an inch wide and a mile deep are recursive and overlapping, just like the writing process.

If you make flexible use of my Chapter 2—or any other—framework for teaching grammatical concepts, if you avoid rigid prescriptions while taking advantage of what other teachers have learned through experience, you may soon find yourself joining Rebecca Schipper in saying, "Consider me sold on the idea of intertwining grammar with writing."

Other quick ideas for launching the teaching of absolutes

1. Have students compose an "I am" poem in which all lines but the first consist of an absolute phrase (create your own model).

2. Have students compose a "boast" poem with absolutes, like this:

My car is a sleek gray cat,

its paws leaping forward the instant I accelerate,
its engine purring contentedly.

3. Have students imitate model sentences in which the absolute describes or narrates. (This activity works especially well when the model sentence comes from a literary work they are reading.) Here are some examples from Ralph Ellison's *Invisible Man* (1952):

I saw the giant bend and clutch the posts at the top of the stairs with both hands, bracing himself, his body gleaming bare in his white shorts.

Before me, in the panel where a mirror is usually placed, I could see a scene from a bullfight, the bull charging close to the man and the man swinging the red cape in sculptured folds so close to his body that man and bull seemed to blend in one swirl of calm, pure motion.

Another example is the opening stanza of W. B. Yeats' "Leda and the Swan" (1924), in which the absolutes hover above the main clause, just as the swan initially hovers above the girl:

A sudden blow: the great wings beating still
Above the staggering girl, her thighs caressed
By the dark webs, her nape caught in his bill,
He holds her breast upon his breast.

A final word

For decades, I have taught the use of detail by having students write poems, even in college classes designed to teach informative and persuasive writing. I've done so because it's easier to focus on using details in a very short piece of writing and because students are quickly able to produce something of which they can be proud. In many college freshman classes, I've first had students create poems in which each line refers to one of the five senses: for example, a poem in which each separate line tells how popped popcorn sounds, looks, feels, smells, and tastes. Pineapples are also excellent for this activity. In fact, I once worked with a group of potential elementary teachers to create a publication we titled *Another Day, Another Pineapple*.

My points here are fourfold:

1. For some—perhaps many—classes at all grade levels, focusing on sensory detail and the use of precise nouns, verbs, adjectives, and adverbs may be an important prelude to playing around with more sophisticated modifying constructions.

2. Activities appropriate for elementary students are often equally appropriate for students at higher levels—and starting with concrete objects is often best.

3. The same procedures for introducing modifying constructions apply when teaching sensory poems or the use of details in other kinds of poems: That is, start with models, compose as a class, and at least consider having students compose in groups before drafting their individual poems.

4. Working with details in poetry and then in narrative/descriptive prose is excellent preparation for writing informative and persuasive prose. Somehow the idea of being specific in other kinds of writing seems easier to grasp after students have written satisfyingly rich poems and narratives.

Why else do I focus on using narrative/descriptive detail in this book? Authors of magazine articles, essays, and nonfiction books are employing these modifying constructions more and more, as the impetus to write from a first-person point of view in these genres has increased and as some of our best science writers—Carl Sagan and Loren Eisley, for instance—have used modifying details that draw readers to their works. Nowadays university English departments may even have classes in creative nonfiction.

Francis Christensen's (1967) words from decades ago ring even more true today:

To begin this discipline [of reconciling inner and outer worlds through writing], and it is discipline, the best form of writing is narration and description, what we may call representational writing in contrast to discursive and persuasive. It is best because it is close to the child's experience; it is concrete and the problem of invention reduces itself to observation. . . . The idea of rhetoric as generative [generating ideas as well as language] makes it possible to teach the sentence as professionals use it, and to teach it positively and creatively.

Still, we should not confuse means and ends. Narrations and descriptions, words and sentences, are means. The end is to enhance life—to give the self (the soul) body by wedding it to the world, to give the world life by wedding it to the self. Or, more simply, to teach to see, for that, as Conrad maintained, is everything. (pp. xi–xii)

When students try to produce the kind of construction you're teaching but produce something else instead, praise them for the construction they've created before showing again what you are aiming for. I find, for example, that when teaching the absolute, I may get some participial phrases instead, especially if I've taught that construction first. Another example: When teaching appositives, you may get some out-of-order adjectives instead—or the other way around, depending upon what you've taught previously. Keep in mind your overall purpose, which is to help students generate more effective sentences and master new constructions. To that end, guide students gently in doing so instead of criticizing them for creating the "wrong" construction. Anticipate, too, that there will be other errors as students experiment with these constructions; most often, for instance, students may forget the comma (or commas) that set off the modifier. In short, remember that we all make new kinds of errors as we try new things, and respond to students as you would like others to respond to you!

If you make the experimentation fun for both you and the students, you'll be surprised at the positive results.

5 Teaching Editing Skills and (Gasp!) Standardized Tests of Grammar Skills

Today's smart teachers have learned that red-inking (or blue-inking or green-inking) students' papers with corrections is not an effective way to teach editing skills. But the swing of the pendulum back toward teaching grammar has brought with it increased pressure to teach numerous editing skills. We must resist. We do not have to repeat either of the devastating learning experiences of this unnamed teacher:

> My own research has convinced me that red-inking errors in students' papers does no good and causes a great many students to hate and fear writing more than anything else they do in school. I gave a long series of tests covering 580 of the most common and persistent errors in usage, diction, and punctuation and 1,000 spelling errors to students in grades 9–12 in many schools, and the average rate of improvement in ability to detect these errors turned out to be 2 percent per year. The dropout rate is more than enough to account for this much improvement in ability to detect these errors if the teachers had not even been there. . . .
>
> When I consider how many hours of my life I have wasted in trying to root out these errors by a method that clearly did not work, I want to kick myself. Any rat that persisted in pressing the wrong lever 10,000 times would be regarded as stupid. I must have gone on pressing it at least 20,000 times without visible effect. (Farrell 1971, p. 141)

We now know that we must teach a limited number of editing skills in conjunction with the writing process, and teach them an inch wide and a mile deep. But how do we decide exactly what skills to focus on?

Deciding what editing skills to teach

The short answer is to teach what our students' writing suggests they need most. All too often, though, we haven't analyzed our students' writing to see what they need but instead have taught our pet peeves, whether they are major issues or not. My own pet peeves in the writing of upper-level college and graduate students are these: using the wrong spelling for homophones like *its/it's* and *their/their/there*; spellings like *would of* for *would have* and *should of* for *should have*; confusion about the uses of *affect* versus *effect*; using the apostrophe in nonpossessive nouns and even in verbs (*he run's*); comma splices; and lack of parallelism. I want students to avoid the first three kinds of errors because they are so distracting, but do they warrant much teaching time and effort? No. On the other hand, avoiding comma splices and using parallelism (and avoiding unparallel constructions in a series) both warrant more instructional time.

So perhaps we can include some of our pet peeves in our list of what to teach, but we have to be careful. After conducting a massive study of teachers' marking of student errors, Connors and Lunsford (1988) found:

> Teachers' ideas about error definition and classification have always been absolute products of their times and cultures. . . .
> Teachers have always marked different phenomena as errors, called them different things, given them differing weights. Error-pattern study is essentially the examination of an ever-shifting pattern of skills judged by an ever-shifting pattern of prejudices. (p. 399)

Wow. Do you as an English teacher (or perhaps even as an intern teacher) feel justifiably indicted? I certainly do.

Are there any research studies or other factors that can help us draw on more than our own pet peeves in making decisions about what editing skills to teach? Yes, up to a point. Of course, examining our own students' editing needs is the best strategy of all.

Maxine Hairston's landmark study (1981) sought to determine what kinds of writing errors were responded to most negatively by businesspeople who were responsible for hiring company employees. Though her methodology was less than ideal, no one questions that certain kinds of errors are "status marking": that is, they tend to suggest that the person is uneducated, whether or not this is true. Here is Hairston's list of status-marking errors, based on her selective questionnaire:

- Nonstandard verb forms in a past or past participle: *brung* instead of *brought*; *had went* instead of *had gone*.
- Lack of subject-verb agreement: *we was* instead of *we were*; *Jones don't think it's acceptable* instead of *Jones doesn't think it's acceptable*.
- Double negatives: *There has never been no one here*; *state employees can't hardly expect a raise*.
- Objective pronoun as subject: *Him and Richard were the last ones hired*.

Clearly these grammatical constructions would suggest to middle-class America that the writer is uneducated or undereducated. Writers need to learn to eliminate these errors from informational and persuasive writing that's to be made public. A longer "shopping list" of such items can be found in Wheeler and Swords (2006), described in Section D1 of the

Grammar Planner. (There I also briefly allude to the successful teaching method they describe in their book.)

What other editing issues might we be well advised to address? As previously mentioned, Connors and Lunsford (1988) undertook a large-scale study to determine which "errors" college teachers of writing marked most often. Jeff Anderson cited the top twenty in Figure 2–7. Below I've divided these twenty errors into categories. Much to my surprise, many of them deal with the use of commas:

Punctuation

- Missing comma after an introductory element
- Missing comma in a compound sentence
- Comma splice
- Missing comma in a series
- Missing comma(s) with a nonrestrictive element
- Unnecessary comma(s) with a restrictive element
- Sentence fragment
- Fused sentence
- Missing or misplaced possessive apostrophe

Verb and pronoun issues

- Lack of agreement between subject and verb
- Lack of agreement between pronoun and antecedent
- Wrong tense or verb form
- Wrong or missing verb ending
- Unnecessary shift in tense
- Unnecessary shift in pronoun
- Vague pronoun reference

Other

- Wrong word
- Wrong or missing preposition
- Misplaced or dangling modifier
- *Its/it's* confusion

A more recent study by Kantz and Yates (1994) used methodology much more likely to produce an accurate picture of college teachers' reactions to various kinds of errors than the Connors and Lunsford study. Kantz and Yates presented college teachers with a well-designed survey that covered twenty-nine different kinds of errors, including eleven errors with homophones like *its/it's*, *their/there*, and *affect/effect*, or with commonly misspelled words. The errors in the sentences (78 items, 6 containing no errors) were not specified, but respondents were asked to mark on a 6-point scale their response to whatever error they identified (or thought they did). A rating of 6 equaled "highly irritating," while 0 equaled "no irritation." The survey was returned and completed correctly by 141 faculty members from various disciplines.

62

5: Teaching Editing Skills and (Gasp!) Standardized Tests of Grammar Skills

While there were significant differences among individuals and certain groups in the responses (e.g., women identified the errors much more accurately than men), there was a definite hierarchy of errors. Certain of them were consistently among the more irritating: The top five were nonstandard verb forms, confusion between *you're* and *your*, confusion between *their* and *there*, sentence fragments, and subject-verb agreement. (As you can see, the more irritating items do not necessarily warrant the most instructional time.)

Overall the survey included four facets of comma use: the comma splice (which ranked 18 in severity), failure to use commas with parenthetical or nonrestrictive elements (ranked 27), no comma in a compound sentence (ranked 29), and no comma after an introductory element (ranked 33). (The latter two issues were rated less irritating than two of the error-free sentences that were misperceived as having errors!)

Kantz and Yates conclude not only that there is "cross-disciplinary agreement about a hierarchy of error" but also that the individual differences in identifying—and misidentifying—errors suggest that "the lack of accuracy in doing the survey means that we should perhaps express our judgments about correctness with a bit of humility."

Taking into account such studies but not being enslaved by them, we still have to make choices about what editing skills to teach. If many or most of our students use status-marking features in their writing, are we going to leap into teaching them the finer points of comma use? Definitely not. We have to prioritize, based on our knowledge of our students' most serious needs. Unfortunately, the makers of the ACT English tests—analyzed in this chapter—may have been highly influenced by the Connors and Lunsford study, which many teachers of English (as well as other disciplines) believe overstates concerns about comma use.

Using appropriate connecting words and the associated punctuation is another crucial issue, especially for teaching informational and persuasive writing—and these kinds of things are tested the most heavily of all on the ACT. Why didn't any of these factors show up on the Connors and Lunsford list? It's my hunch—and theirs too—that the items marked most often by college teachers were simply the items they found easiest to mark! We must keep this in mind and not limit our teaching of editing skills to Connors and Lunsford's top twenty—though they should be included if your state, like Jeff Anderson's Texas, tests those skills. Instead of emphasizing them, teach the more important skills that make ideas, sentences, paragraphs, and whole pieces of writing flow logically, with appropriate punctuation.

Teaching revision and editing skills for the standardized tests

First, we need an accurate picture of what our students are being tested on. Once in a teacher workshop, someone objected that teaching adjectival phrases as I was recommending wouldn't help his students identify parts of speech on the state test. Fortunately I had done my homework and knew that his state didn't test the ability to identify or label grammatical elements. Extra fortunately, someone from the state department of education was there to reinforce the point and explain with all her authority what *was* tested: writing and, to some extent, the use of editing conventions as part of holistic scoring. She also backed up my assertion—based on their state writing rubric, which I had projected on a transparency— that helping students expand sentences with modifying details would address the rubric categories of idea development, style/voice, and sentence sense/fluency.

This story has a happy ending: When I ran into this young teacher again a couple of months later at the National Council of Teachers of English convention, he told me he'd been teaching some of those adjectival constructions, with wonderful results in students' writing. But the story should serve as a warning: *Don't assume what your students will be tested on; find out!* The ACT and SAT tests of revision and editing skills, for instance, are just that: They, too, do not require identifying any kind of grammatical element or construction by name.

Should we even try to teach to the tests?

My quick response to that is yes—and no. Let me explain. As caring and responsible teachers, we can't just ignore the tests. They are a reality and, sadly, a factor by which not only our students but also we—and our schools and school systems—will be evaluated. Still, what to do, what to do? Here are suggestions, balancing the current mania for assessment with the need to reserve most of our instructional time for productive instruction in the various aspects of writing.

1. Don't abandon best practice in the teaching of writing (or the teaching of writing entirely!) in favor of test preparation. It doesn't help anyway—especially if actual writing is assessed and you take time away from the teaching of writing to teach skills tested on multiple choice tests.

2. Make the most of the overlap between the revision and editing skills your students really need and the skills tested on the standardized tests. There are too many kinds of items tested on the ACT and SAT, for example, to reasonably teach them all during the writing process—and many of your students may have little need for some of those skills as writers. Those students motivated enough to learn the finer points of editing skills can be given special help and directed to grammar books they can study—and/or to the explanations in practice test books.

3. Reserve for test preparation sessions the items that seem relatively unimportant to your students, not only as writers but also as test takers. (This may require some investigation into what the tests do and don't emphasize.) Skills that students consider irrelevant are rarely retained

Don't assume what your students will be tested on; find out!

64

5: Teaching Editing Skills and (Gasp!) Standardized Tests of Grammar Skills

for long, and skills that are taught in isolation are rarely retained anyway, by most of our students. This double whammy suggests last-minute teaching may be best.

4. Do use practice tests or test items with students. Without severely curtailing the teaching of writing in order to teach to any test of English skills, make the practice proportionate to the difficulty of the test and its importance in student assessment. For example, Michigan has decided to use the ACT as its overall assessment instrument in the junior year. Frankly, I think the test is difficult, both in content and in the multiple-choice format, which can often trick even good student editors—and their teachers—into answering incorrectly. Some experience with practice tests *and the skills assessed* will be necessary.

5. Don't limit your students' writing or your teaching of writing to the "rules" tested on these large-scale tests. The tests are extremely conservative with regard to grammar. They test "rules" that many or most published writers don't follow, "errors" that aren't considered errors by most publishers, and "no-nos" that never should have found their way into English grammar books in the first place, since they were based on the structure of Latin rather than English—or simply made up by the books' writers. Teach students to write like published authors and then teach the standardized tests' "rules" as part of test preparation. Students are usually able to understand the need to do things differently under different circumstances: After all, they've been doing that for years, when this year's English teacher has expectations different from last year's or Mom's expectations are different from Dad's. You might try giving students credit for being able to "code switch" from good writing to successful test taking.

6. Always keep firmly in mind that even excellent writers, even excellent editors of their own writing, may not be able to do well on such multiple-choice tests of writing skills.

With these recommendations as background, I'll informally analyze the ACT English test as an example of how teachers can come to better understand the demands of any standardized test of writing skills that their students might be required to take. (Obviously not every teacher needs to do this individually; it could be done at the grade, school, system, or even state level, as relevant.)

Inside the ACT: What's heavily tested and what isn't?

First, to reinforce the last point, consider what the Princeton Review's *Cracking the ACT* (2005) practice book bluntly admits:

> No matter how well or how poorly you do on the English test, you should not feel that your ACT English score truly represents your ability to write. . . . We don't mean that ACT is doing a bad

job. It's tough to measure English skills, and we think the test writers have constructed a fair test. In the end, however, what the ACT English test measures is how well you take the ACT English test. (p. 25)

Enough said?

In an attempt to help teachers in my state understand the ACT's multiple-choice questions on writing skills, I examined several practice books from 2005 and 2006. I particularly liked *The* Real *ACT Prep Guide* (ACT, 2005) because it was written by the test makers and included tests previously given. Also, I found the *The New ACT* (SparkNotes, 2005) breakdown on the division and subdivision of items on the ACT revealing:

Usage/mechanics questions (40 items)
    Punctuation (10)
    Basic grammar and usage (12) (but *not labeling* any aspects of grammar)
    Sentence structure (18)
Rhetorical skills questions (35 total)
    Writing strategy questions (12)
    Organization (11)
    Style (12)

This was a good start, I thought, yet still not specific enough to be really helpful to teachers and students.

So I analyzed all the items in six tests (two previous real ones and four practice ones), which was more difficult than I imagined, because two or three skills might be tested at once. Here, from *The* Real *ACT Prep Guide* (2005, p. 154), is a fairly common example of a complex test item. The underlined portion of the sentence is the part addressed by the four options:

<u>Down the street from the college, I attend,</u> the Save-U Laundromat is always open and someone is always there.

Options:
    F. NO CHANGE
    G. college, I attend
    H. college I attend,
    I.   college I attend

While test takers may indeed get the question right through a hunch or their intuitive sentence sense, the question is designed to test two things: recognition that *I attend* is a restrictive clause that shouldn't be separated by a comma from *college*, the preceding noun that it modifies; and recognition that, on the other hand, a comma is needed after *attend*, which concludes the introductory phrase. The correct answer is H, but how best to categorize the question? Sometimes I put a question in more than one category.

66

5: Teaching Editing Skills and (Gasp!) Standardized Tests of Grammar Skills

It proved difficult to generalize about the kinds of items tested because the frequency of some items varied considerably from one practice test to another (though there was more consistency among the previous real tests in the ACT's own guide). Also, I'm sure I did not always characterize the items the way the test makers did, because I did not come up with the requisite number of items in the categories offered by the SparkNotes book (2005).

Keeping all this in mind, plus the fact that this is only one teacher's analysis of six tests, I nevertheless think the following breakdown of items is quite helpful. Mostly, of course, it's helpful to teachers whose students are all going to be required to take the ACT. But it should also be useful in suggesting some of the kinds of editing skills that really should be taught; it's a corrective to the limitations of Connors and Lunsford's top twenty. Moreover, this analysis suggests the kind of breakdown you and your colleagues might do on another standardized test, such as the SAT. (I was tempted to include even more detail about the relative frequencies I found, but the more detailed, the greater the likelihood that the patterns won't carry over to future tests.)

If you feel intimidated or overwhelmed by terms and concepts that you don't understand, keep in mind that the Grammar Planner in Part 2 briefly discusses most of these issues and that the most esoteric-sounding items are sometimes the least important to teach.

Rhetorical skills: Content, organization, connection, and flow—highest emphasis

Together, these rhetorical skills received by far the greatest emphasis.

All the passages on the ACT tests are informative, with or without a persuasive edge. They vary in degree of formality and tone. Within that context, what the ACT calls "rhetorical skills" includes nearly half of the test items: 35 out of 75. Even though the way I characterized test items sometimes produced fewer than 35 in this category, in almost every test I examined, this category received the greatest emphasis. Repeatedly, there were items dealing with these issues:

- Order of sentences within a paragraph
- Order of paragraphs within the whole piece
- Topic of the passage
- Consistent focus of the passage on the topic
- Whether and/or where to add a sentence giving details
- Deletion of a redundant or irrelevant sentence
- Sentences to make transitions within paragraphs

Questions on transitions within and between clauses, sentences, and paragraphs were so numerous that they are also listed as a separate category, as follows.

Connectors, punctuation, and sentence structure relating to flow—high emphasis

While relating to meaning, organization, and flow, each of the following were major categories themselves and received substantial attention.

- Brevity: that is, eliminating wordiness
- Comma use, including numerous questions requiring elimination of commas when no specific rule requires their use (I have included comma splice sentences in this category)
- Connectors:
  - Choices appropriate to meaning and/or sequencing or logical flow
  - Choice between kind of connective word or phrase, given the grammatical structure and punctuation
- Ordering of elements within sentences for clarity and flow (includes items on "misplaced" or "dangling" modifiers, both of which occurred rarely)

Phrase-level and sentence-level constraints—moderate emphasis

These items received moderate emphasis.

Some of these items—especially parallelism—were assessed frequently on one practice test, but less often on others. The categories are listed in descending order of importance:

- Verb tense or form, with many questions focusing on consistency of tense as appropriate to fit with other verbs or overall tense of the passage
- Subject-verb agreement, under varied circumstances
- Ordering of sentence elements for clarity and flow, including "misplaced" or (rarely) "dangling" modifiers
- Parallelism, especially of verb tenses, sometimes of noun forms

Phrase-level and sentence-level constraints—low emphasis

These items received low emphasis.

- Pronoun issues as an entire category, including agreement in number with antecedent, appropriate case, and appropriate person
- Sentence fragments, along with grammatically malformed and therefore incomplete sentences (these were clearly awkward and ineffective fragments)

Phrase-level and sentence-level constraints—minimal emphasis

Few, if any of these items were directly assessed on any given test. In fact, there were probably no more than a half dozen of all these items taken together.

68

5: Teaching Editing Skills and (Gasp!) Standardized Tests of Grammar Skills

- Adjective or adverb issues: choice of adjective or adverb form to modify a noun or verb; choice between commonly confused adjective and adverb forms; conventional comparative or superlative forms
- Avoidance of double negatives like *can't hardly, won't never*
- Uses of punctuation other than the comma, including:
  - Colon (few items on appropriate or inappropriate use, but many more instances of a colon as a wrong choice in a comma question)
  - Semicolon (same distribution as with colon)
  - Everything else as one category: apostrophes in possessives and not in simple plurals or verbs; dashes, parentheses, and such (periods, exclamation marks, and question marks were almost never tested directly)
- Other word issues:
  - Choice of spellings for a homophone (*there/their/they're*; *its/it's*)
  - Choice between *that* or *which* to introduce an adjective clause
  - Choice between *who* or *whom*
  - Choice between commonly confused pairs (*affect/effect*)
  - Choice of preposition within idiomatic expressions
  - Choice of "standard" past tense or past participle forms (not *brung* for past tense)

What aspects of editing should we teach in the context of writing?

This decision needs to take into account various factors:

1. What aspects of editing will help the overall quality of students' writing the most? Perhaps the "rhetorical" skills tested on the ACT?
2. Do your students need help in learning to code-switch from their informal language to the formal language considered acceptable in the marketplace? If so, such issues need attention before the kinds of editing issues that Connors and Lunsford found were marked the most by college teachers.
3. Do your students' writings exhibit mostly the editing issues listed in Connors and Lunsford's top twenty?
4. How important is it for your students to focus on eliminating wordiness and redundancy, as stressed in the ACT?

As you think about these issues and use the Grammar Planner, keep in mind that we cannot do it all. We really do have to prioritize.

The Grammar Planner

As smart teachers, we realize it's better that little yellow grammar modules *don't* rain down from the sky, no matter how much we might wistfully yearn for such "weather." We can judiciously draw examples and ideas from various resources, though, including some grammar sites found on the Web, if we keep in mind what research and recent experimentation suggest:

1. Teaching grammar in isolation doesn't improve writing—nor does teaching a grammar book, including this Grammar Planner. (See the York study [Andrews et al., 2004b], which was described in Chapter 1.)

2. Teaching everything amounts to teaching nothing, while teaching fewer things deeply and in the context of writing holds more promise for long-term gains.

3. Teaching less grammar but teaching options and skills *as we help students use these tools* to enrich and enhance their writing can generate stronger and more interesting writing, as well as writing that meets the conventional expectations of the marketplace.

4. Teaching grammatical analysis (such as determining subject and verb, for agreement) warrants much less time than producing sentences with interesting details, organizing and combining elements within and beyond sentences, and establishing appropriate tone for purpose and audience.

5. Testing the naming of parts is not necessary, and indeed contraindicated and counterproductive, even though we and our students may be using a few grammatical terms in discussion.

6. Good writing does not necessarily follow all the grammar-book rules, so teaching students to write well and teaching them to perform well on standardized tests are not synonymous and should, to some extent, be separate instructional enterprises (a point to be demonstrated more fully in Section D).

When these principles guide our teaching of grammar for writing, it is much more likely to be successful. *We* are more likely to be successful, and *our students* are more likely to be successful as writers.

How can the following Grammar Planner help you as a teacher? First, it can help you understand the structure of the language if you have little or no background in English grammar. This is important, because best-practice teaching doesn't play it safe by teaching grammar books with answer keys. Teachers need to be able to answer students' questions about grammar as well as plan and teach lessons directly relating grammar to writing and perhaps literature. Engaging in close encounters of the third grammatical kind requires us to know more than we plan to teach, as we start helping students enrich their writing by using modifying constructions and parallelism. In particular, we need to know more in order to teach editing skills. Second, the Planner is designed to nudge you into considering whether certain topics need to be taught at all and, if so, within what genres and during what aspects of the writing process. It may be best to teach some skills only in preparation for standardized tests, if then.

Here are some questions to provoke thoughtful decision making:

1. What aspects of grammar do your students already command in their writing? Even if a grammatical construction or skill is listed in your state or local standards for your grade level, do you really need to teach that construction or skill for writing, or do students' writings already demonstrate its use?

2. What aspects of grammar for enriching writing—such as modifiers and the use of parallelism—will your students most benefit from?

3. What editing skills do *your* students most need to learn as writers— and in what areas do these needs dovetail with the standards and/or with skills assessed on a standardized test, if your students are required to take one?

4. What editing skills are so minor, and what kinds of errors occur so infrequently, that you can justifiably omit them from what you teach during the writing process?

5. What is actually tested on the state or standardized test(s) used in your state, district, or school, and what additional aspects of grammar will you need to review as part of preparing students to take such a test or tests?

Whether you're making these decisions individually or as part of a committee, the Planner can help.

This Grammar Planner section has been designed to make it easy to record your decisions about teaching grammar. The wide column in the outer margin is for indicating the writing phase or phases during which you'll teach a concept—if you plan to teach it in conjunction with writing. At each new section is a yes/no option to indicate whether you plan to review the concept for test-taking. There is plenty of space for you to make other notes as well.

Do keep in mind, however, that simply teaching the Grammar Planner as a text to be mastered is not the best way to help students *use* the resources of the language in their writing. They need the kinds of teaching described in Part 1, namely, to teach grammar "an inch wide and a mile deep."

Grammar to Expand and Enrich Writing

Putting First Things First

A

Addressing ideas, voice, sentence fluency, and conventions (adding, placing, reordering, and punctuating modifiers and parallel elements)

This section on modifiers and parallelism precedes the section on the sentence in order to emphasize the point that we need to help students elaborate on content and write effective sentences before we address editing. In other words, the Grammar Planner begins with grammatical options rather than conventions. You may find it useful to review the basic grammatical definitions in Chapter 3 before approaching this section—or to look ahead at Section B. Note that the issues listed below each section title refer to categories in the six traits of writing system (Spandel, 2005; Culham, 2003).

Adverbials, being less complicated than adjectivals, are discussed first.

A1 adverbials

An *adverbial* is any single-word adverb or adverbial phrase or clause—that is, any word or group of words—that describes the verb or the whole subject-plus-verb as a unit. Adverbials usually tell *how, when, where,* or *why* with respect to an action. The *how* category includes in what manner, by what means, how far, how long (for what length of time), and so forth, but always in relation to an action rather than a person or thing.

Use a comma after an introductory adverbial element if you want your reader to make a substantial pause.

> Cautiously, Amanda turned the knob and opened the door.

> Three years later, the bridge was completed.

> In the middle of nowhere, our car suddenly sputtered and died.

> Thanks to their heroic efforts, not one piece of furniture was scratched.

Review for Test?	Y	N

Phase of writing process in which to teach:

To make my sentences flow more smoothly, I often move adverbial modifiers to the front of the sentence when editing my writing.

Clara's directions being vague, we got lost almost immediately.

Whenever you have the time, please come for a week to visit.

Notice that the internal structure of an adverbial can be almost anything, even a nominal (*three years later*), but it's the external function of the group of words that makes it adverbial.

Some handbooks offer arbitrary advice like "use a comma if the introductory adverbial is five words or longer," which means that not all introductory adverbial phrases require a comma after them. In practice, authors usually put a comma after a shorter introductory element, too, if they want their readers to pause.

Review for Test?   Y   N

Phase of writing process
in which to teach:

A1-a **adverbial clauses**

A *clause* consists of a subject + a complete (or properly formed) verb. An *adverb clause* (*adverbial clause*) works like an adverb, to modify the verb or the main subject-plus-verb unit. Adverbial clauses are dependent on a main clause; they usually tell when or why (*after, because,* etc.), indicate under what condition, or express contrast with respect to the major action.

Sometimes an adverbial is almost a clause, but not quite: Notice, for example, the underlined construction in *Clara's directions being vague, we got lost almost immediately.* This underlined part does not fit the requirement for a clause, adverbial or otherwise, because the verb is not properly formed: *being* cannot stand alone as a verb.

We can make an independent clause into a subordinate (dependent) one simply by putting a subordinating conjunction in front of it. The clause must then ordinarily be attached to the preceding or following main clause.

He bought lottery tickets every week. He never won anything.

although he bought lottery tickets every week

Possible resulting sentences:

He never won anything, *although* he bought lottery tickets every week.

Although he bought lottery tickets every week, he never won anything.

Notice that a comma is required after an introductory subordinate clause. The comma is usually—but not always—omitted before a final adverbial clause. A comma was included in the first of the previous pair of sentences to signal a significant pause, giving the reader time to think about the main clause before going on to the subordinate *although* clause.

Published writers sometimes punctuate a subordinate clause as if it were a complete sentence when it is clear from the preceding context: *I benefit from exercising.* <u>*When I do it*</u>. Stylistically, this strategy can sometimes be effective. But on standardized tests, punctuating a subordinate clause as a complete sentence (*Although he bought lottery tickets every week.*) will be considered wrong. In either case, the writer has created a sentence fragment.

WORDS THAT COMMONLY FUNCTION AS SUBORDINATING CONJUNCTIONS
(some have other functions as well)

TIME	CAUSE	CONDITION	CONTRAST
after	as	as if	although
as	because	assuming that	even though
as soon as	in order that	if	rather than
before	since	in case	though
since	so that	unless	whereas
till		when	while
until		whether	
when			
while			

A1-b movable adverbials

Adverbial modifiers are often moved from one place in a sentence to another in order to make the sentence flow more smoothly. Such modifiers frequently set the stage for the main subject + verb unit and therefore are best placed at or near the beginning of the sentence.

I often move an adverbial modifier to the front of a sentence, <u>in order to make it flow more smoothly</u>.

<u>To make my sentences flow more smoothly</u>, I often move an adverbial modifier to the front of the sentence.

<u>To set the stage for what I want to emphasize</u>, I often move an adverbial modifier to the front of the sentence.

<u>When editing my writing</u>, I often move adverbial modifiers to the front of a sentence, in order to make it flow more smoothly or to set the stage for what I want to emphasize.

Authors often move adverbial modifiers to the beginning of a sentence <u>in both narrative and explanatory writing</u>, to set the stage for what is to come.

<u>In both narrative and explanatory writing</u>, authors often move adverbial modifiers to the beginning of a sentence, to set the stage for what is to come.

You'd better hurry up <u>if you want to go to lunch with me</u>.

<u>If you want to go to lunch with me</u>, you'd better hurry up.

I'll even treat you to lunch, <u>as soon as I finish this last paragraph</u>.

<u>As soon as I finish this last paragraph</u>, I'll even treat you to lunch.

"Fronting" some modifiers is especially helpful when the sentence includes several adverbials needed for clarity.

Adverbial modifiers that are movable can be considered "free" modifiers, whether or not they are set off by commas.

A2 adjectivals that are "bound" modifiers

An *adjectival* is any single-word adjective or adjectival phrase or clause—that is, a word or group of words—that describes and is said to "modify" a noun. Often, but not always, single-word adjectivals occur right before the noun they modify. Otherwise, they typically occur after a form of the verb *to be*: *am, is, are, was, were, been, being*, or *be* itself. In both situations they are "bound" to the noun they modify.

They pulled up the <u>enormous</u> turnip.

My terrier snuggled comfortably in his <u>warm</u> bed.

The protestors hugged the <u>gnarled</u> tree trunks.

Gravity is the <u>dominating</u> force.

I am <u>tired</u>, <u>hungry</u>, and <u>sleepy</u>. (Three single-word adjectivals in a series.)

Grover is absolutely <u>starved</u>. (Single-word adjectival modified by *absolutely*.)

That solution will be <u>fine</u>.

Usually, single words that can work as adjectivals will fit comfortably into this test frame: The [noun] is very _____.

Words that can introduce a noun are called *noun determiners*. These include the articles *a*, *an*, and *the*; the possessives *my, our, your, his*, *her*, *its*, *their*; the demonstratives *this*, *that*, *these*, *those*; and number words like *six* or *sixth*. None of these words can fit into the adjective test slot.

A2-a **adjectival clauses**

An *adjective clause* (*adjectival clause*) is a complete subject-verb unit that describes or "modifies" a noun.

The adjectival clause is introduced by *that* if the clause is essential to clarify what entity is being talked about; *that* clauses are called *restrictive*, because they limit or restrict the entity, telling which one is being specified by the noun.

> Throw the ball to the player *that is not paying attention.* (*Who* would more commonly be used, but *that* emphasizes the player's robotic state.)
>
> The toys *that she's tired of* can be put away for now.
>
> The motor *that's in my little car* isn't powerful enough.

Sometimes the *that* can be omitted:

> The toys she's tired of can be put away for now.

Also, a whole clause can often be reduced to just a phrase, with no complete subject-verb unit:

> The motor in my little car isn't powerful enough.

See Section C2-b1 for fuller treatment of the relative pronouns that relate an adjective clause to the noun they modify.

A2-b **other postnoun adjectivals that are "bound"**

Both essential and nonessential adjectival clauses are "bound" to the noun they modify, in that they must occur after the noun.

Sometimes modifiers are essential to clarify the meaning of a preceding noun (or pronoun) and are therefore bound to it in the additional sense that there is no comma separating the noun from its modifier. As conceptualized by the writer, all of the following underlined clauses or phrases are required to clarify the noun, answering the question "which one?"

Review for Test? **Y** **N**

Phase of writing process in which to teach:

Review for Test? **Y** **N**

Phase of writing process in which to teach:

Clause:

> That cell phone <u>that's ringing</u> can't be mine.

> They couldn't contact the miners <u>who were trapped deep within the mine.</u>

Words or phrases, each of which could be viewed as a reduction of an entire adjectival clause:

> That cell phone <u>bleating so loudly</u> can't be mine.

> The cell phone <u>playing "Greensleeves"</u> is mine.

> They couldn't contact the miners <u>trapped deep within the mine.</u>

> Fraternity rush week is the week <u>most feared.</u>

> That's the one <u>meant.</u>

> I want to purchase only the onions <u>in that bin.</u>

> The guy <u>from Nigeria</u> is my new best friend.

Review for Test?   Y   N

Phase of writing process
in which to teach:

A3 prepositional phrases: adjectival and adverbial

The last two examples in the preceding list are *prepositional phrases*. A preposition occurs before a nominal; hence *pre-position*, or *preposition*. Together, the preposition and the nominal constitute a prepositional phrase that modifies the noun before it:

> Those magazines <u>on the floor</u> can be thrown out.

> The flowers <u>outside the border</u> should be replanted.

> The border <u>of the garden</u> is meant to contain the planted flowers.

> I don't like the fence <u>around our yard.</u>

Each of the prepositional phrases tells which one or which ones. They function adjectivally, to modify the preceding noun.

In context, many prepositional phrases function like adverbs, not like adjectives. When a prepositional phrase functions adverbially it tells *how* (by what means, in what manner, how far, how long, etc.), *when, where,* or *why* with respect to the action.

> Stack the magazines; don't throw them <u>on the floor</u>. (Tells where not to throw the magazines.)

> Don't plant those flowers <u>outside the border of the garden</u>. (Contains within it an adjectival prepositional phrase modifying <u>border</u>.)

Macauley can help install the fencing <u>around our yard</u>. (Tells where the fencing is to be installed.)

Writers do not need to identify whether a prepositional phrasae is working adjectivally or adverbially. However, the distinction is a grammatical curiosity that might arise in discussion.

WORDS COMMONLY USED AS PREPOSITIONS
(several function in other ways, too)

about	beside	from	outside	toward
above	besides	in	over	under
across	between	inside	past	underneath
after	beyond	into	plus	unlike
against	but	like	regarding	until
along	by	near	respecting	unto
among	concerning	next to	round	up
around	considering	of	since	upon
as	despite	off	than	with
at	down	on	through	without
before	during	onto	throughout	
behind	except	opposite	till	
below	for	out	to	

A4 adjectivals that are "free" modifiers

In 1967, rhetorician Francis Christensen pointed out that the modifiers least often used by students—and therefore most in need of instructional coaxing—are grammatically nonessential adjectivals, ones not bound to the nominal they modify. Typically such modifiers occur at the end of the sentence (or clause), at the beginning, or right after the noun they describe. Depending on the meaning and the appropriate flow of ideas, such modifiers may be movable from one to another of these positions in the sentence.

Not bound but "free," such modifiers are set off by a comma or commas. The most common types of potentially "free" adjectival modifiers in published writing are the *appositive*; *out-of-order adjectives* and *adjective-headed phrases* not closely bound to a noun; the unbound *present participial phrase*; and the *absolute*.

A4-a appositives

An *appositive* is a noun, or a nominal with a primary ("head") noun or pronoun, that most commonly comes right after another noun that it

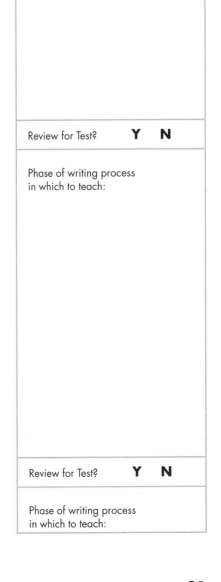

Review for Test?   **Y**   **N**

Phase of writing process in which to teach:

Review for Test?   **Y**   **N**

Phase of writing process in which to teach:

describes. The appositive may be a near synonym for the noun, renaming it in a different way. In many instances the appositive specifies a category into which the modified noun fits. Sometimes it simply elaborates on the modified noun. In every case, an appositive is set off by a comma or commas from the rest of the sentence.

> Sarah's pretend uncle, <u>Marvin K. Mooney</u>, is actually a character in a book, *Marvin K. Mooney, Will You Please Go Now!*

> Marvin K. Mooney, <u>a character created by Dr. Seuss</u>, isn't a relative of mine.

> Marvin K. Mooney, <u>Sarah's pretend uncle</u>, isn't anyone's actual relative.

> <u>A character created by Dr. Seuss</u>, Marvin K. Mooney isn't a relative to be proud of.

> Sarah delights in Marvin K. Mooney, <u>a character in a Dr. Seuss book</u>.

> We bought those notebook folders that were on sale, <u>the ones with weird designs</u>. (Modifies *notebook folders*.)

> The notebook folders with weird designs, <u>the ones on sale</u>, seemed almost psychedelic.

The appositive is a noun or noun phrase in form, though it functions adjectivally to modify another noun. In rare instances, a pronoun could be used instead of the head noun in an appositive: *The notebook folders with weird designs, **those** on sale, looked almost psychedelic.*

Occasionally an appositive occurs before the noun it modifies: *A product of the "me" generation, Garmon thinks of no one but himself.*

A4-b out-of-order adjectivals

Out-of-order adjectivals can be single-word adjectives or adjective-headed phrases. "Out of order" simply means that they do not occur immediately before the noun in the way that most adjectives do; they are set off by a comma or commas.

A4-b1 single-word adjectives

Harry Noden, in *Image Grammar* (1999), has characterized as "adjectives out of order" those adjectives that occur at the beginning of a sentence, right after the noun they modify, or at the end of the sentence (even if they modify the subject). Such adjectives, singly or in pairs or threesomes, are set off from the rest of the sentence by a comma or commas.

Alone, she darted anxiously through the corridor.

My roommate, scared, darted anxiously through the corridor.

My roommate darted anxiously through the corridor, alone and scared.

My doctor, tall and handsome, catches everyone's eye.

Tall and handsome, my doctor catches everyone's eye.

He kept whistling the same tune, catchy but unidentifiable.

Catchy but unidentifiable, that tune haunted me all day.

That tune, catchy but unidentifiable, has haunted me all day.

The coffee was black, bitter, and cold.

A4-b2 adjective-headed phrases

Similarly, adjective-headed phrases may occur in one, two, or all three of those set-off modifying positions.

Aware of her limited time, the surgeon began the delicate operation.

The surgeon began the delicate operation, *aware* of her limited time.

The surgeon, *aware* of her limited time, began the delicate operation.

Agitated after the near-miss, Chris almost rammed the car ahead.

Chris, *agitated* after the near-miss, almost rammed the car ahead.

Planned by their Machiavellian chemistry teacher, the experiment baffled the entire class.

The experiment, *planned* by their Machiavellian chemistry teacher, baffled the entire class.

Broken by the crash, Lamar's left headlight dangled from its socket.

Lamar's left headlight dangled from its socket, *broken* by the crash.

The head "adjectives" in the last four sentences are technically past participles, derived from the form of the verb that is used after *have, has,* or *had*: *The teacher has planned the experiment. The crash had broken the headlight.* However, it hardly seems worthwhile to try to distinguish these from other adjectival phrases.

A4-c **present participle phrases**

Present participial phrases occur frequently in effective writing, whether in narratives or in explanations and persuasive writing. Therefore, they are worth discussing—and teaching—separately.

A *present participle* is simply the *-ing* form of a verb functioning adjectivally. A *present participle phrase* is a group of words functioning the same way, with the *-ing* word as its key element, or "head" word. These are also known as *present **participial** phrases*, meaning that they function the way a present participle does.

Abby leaned over the rail, almost losing her balance.

Laughing and grinning from ear to ear, Abby held up the fish she'd just caught.

Abby, laughing and grinning from ear to ear, held up the fish she'd just caught.

Wondering what had happened, Bo swiveled his head to look.

Bo swiveled his head to look, wondering what had happened.

Bo, wondering what had happened, swiveled his head to look.

Gerunds

When the *-ing* form of a verb works like a noun, it is called a *gerund*.

Skateboarding can be dangerous.

Ginny likes riding her horse Grace. (gerund phrase)

Arguing with me won't get you anywhere. (gerund phrase)

Thus it is the function of an *-ing* word that distinguishes a main verb (*The water is running*) from a participle (*The running water is cool*) from a gerund (*Samantha enjoys running cold water over her toes*).

A4-d **absolutes**

An *absolute* is a phrase that's almost a sentence, but not quite. Typically it could be restored to a full sentence by adding *was* or *were*.

Sometimes the absolute refers back, grammatically, to something in the main clause:

Sandy skated across the pond, her scarf waving behind her.

Scott waved his letter in the air, his arms gesturing excitedly.

Her hair a tangled mess, Imogene shook off groggy sleep.

The crowd waiting to get tickets, <u>their feet tired from standing,</u> finally began to sit on the pavement.

And sometimes the absolute has no grammatical relationship at all to the main clause:

<u>Traffic at a standstill,</u> Paula finally jumped out of the cab and walked.

We walked cautiously down the narrow path, <u>the moonlight showing us the way.</u>

As with other free modifying adjectivals, an absolute can often be moved to at least one other position in a sentence:

<u>His arms open wide,</u> Tyson greeted his grandson.

Tyson greeted his grandson, <u>his arms open wide.</u>

Tyson, <u>his arms open wide,</u> greeted his grandson.

Some of the absolutes in the previous set are also movable.

A5 movable adjectivals revisited

As most of the preceding and all of the following examples illustrate, non-essential, "free" adjectival modifiers will often fit appropriately in two different sentence positions and sometimes in all three: at the beginning of the sentence, right after the noun they modify, or at the end of the sentence.

<u>A natural hitter by anyone's standards,</u> Chuck slammed the ball over the fence.

Chuck, <u>a natural hitter by anyone's standards,</u> slammed the ball over the fence.

The deer stood outside our window, <u>calm and unafraid.</u>

<u>Calm and unafraid,</u> the deer stood outside our window.

The deer, <u>calm and unafraid,</u> stood outside our window.

<u>Happy at the sight of the deer,</u> Alan hunted for the camera.

Alan, <u>happy at the sight of the deer,</u> hunted for the camera.

Belinda smiled engagingly at Carlos, <u>laughing at her foolish mistake.</u>

<u>Laughing at her foolish mistake,</u> Carla smiled engagingly at Carlos.

Carla, <u>laughing at her foolish mistake,</u> smiled engagingly at Carlos.

Review for Test?   **Y   N**

Phase of writing process in which to teach:

His eyes wide with wonder, Juan stared at the gently falling snow.

Juan stared at the gently falling snow, his eyes wide with wonder.

Juan, his eyes wide with wonder, stared at the gently falling snow.

See Part 2, Section B6-a, for more examples.

In the writing of professionals, free modifiers occur most often at the end of the sentence, even when they modify the subject. Alternatively, they often occur at the beginning of a sentence, setting the stage. Such adjectival modifiers occur much less often after the subject and before the verb, as in the last example. In that medial position, they interrupt the flow of the subject-verb unit.

A6 dangling modifiers

When a sentence opens with a group of words that allude to an action but do not specify the actor, the rule is that the subject of the following clause must specify the actor. Put another way, the opening words must modify the subject of the following clause, not some other noun in the sentence. Here are some examples of dangling modifiers and how they might be repaired (there are other possible solutions; these are not exhaustive):

Dangling: Taxiing down the runway, the woman screamed for the plane to stop.

Repaired: As the plane taxied down the runway, the woman screamed for it to stop.

OR   The woman screamed for the plane to stop as it taxied down the runway.

Dangling: Climbing the wall, the school was visible in the distance.

Repaired: Climbing the wall, I could see the school, visible in the distance.

OR   When I climbed the wall, I could see the school, visible in the distance.

OR   I could see the school in the distance after I climbed the wall.

Dangling: When starting the car, the gear shift has to be in "park."

Repaired: When starting the car, be sure the gear shift is still in "park." (There is no specified subject of the main clause, but the "understood" subject is *you*: You are starting the car and making sure the gear shift is in "park.")

Rephrased for logical sequence: Be sure the gear shift is in "park" before you try to start the car.

Grammar to Expand and Enrich Writing

When three or more of the same grammatical elements are used in se-quence, they are said to be parallel. *Parallelism* is often used for emphasis, for impact: to make a point, to shock, to fire the imagination, to inspire, to rouse to action. Abraham Lincoln's powerful Gettysburg address and Martin Luther King's "I have a dream" speech come readily to mind.

The term *parallelism* is usually reserved for a series of three or more of the same (tightly or loosely construed) grammatical constructions in a se-ries, separated by commas. A parallel series might consist of simple sen-tences, simple subjects or other nominals, simple predicates, simple verb phrases, prepositional phrases, participial phrases, absolutes, subordinate clauses, even fragments—in short, any kind of grammatical construction the writer might care to string together. Sometimes parallel items repeat some of the same words, though certainly not always.

The following examples of parallelism come from *Night* (1960), by Elie Wiesel. This is an autobiographical novel based on the author's hor-rific experiences as a Jewish teenager during the Holocaust. Parallelism is especially effective in this novel to underscore the terrible circumstances, events, and pain that the Jews suffered under Hitler's relentless drive to eliminate them:

Several days passed. Several weeks. Several months. Life had re-turned to normal. A wind of calmness and reassurance blew through our houses. The traders were doing good business, the students lived buried in their books, and the children played in the streets. (p. 4)

I had asked my father to sell out, liquidate his business, and leave. (p. 6)

The Germans were already in the town, the Fascists were already in power, the verdict had already been pronounced, yet the Jews of Sighet continued to smile. (pp. 7–8)

We were no longer allowed to go into restaurants or cafes, to travel on the railway, to attend the synagogue, to go out into the street af-ter six o'clock. (p. 9)

Perhaps they thought that God could have devised no torment in hell worse than that of sitting there among the bundles, in the middle of the road, beneath a blazing sun; that anything would be preferable to that. (p. 14)

One by one they passed in front of me, teachers, friends, others, all those I had been afraid of, all those I once could have laughed at, all those I had lived with over the years. They went by, fallen, drag-ging their packs, dragging their lives, deserting their homes, the years of their childhood, cringing like beaten dogs. (pp. 14–15)

What more can one say about the powerful effects of grammatical con-structions used in parallel series?

In a lighter vein, all of the examples below are taken from *Maniac Magee*, by Jerry Spinelli (1990). This engaging story, appropriate for middle schoolers, features realistic characters as well as deeper lessons to ponder.

Pretty soon there were two of everything in the house. <u>Two bathrooms</u>. <u>Two TVs</u>. <u>Two refrigerators</u>. If it were possible, they would have had two Jeffreys. (p. 6)

<u>They stopped</u>, <u>they blinked</u>, <u>they turned</u>, <u>they stared after him</u>, <u>they wondered</u>: *Do I know that kid?* (p. 9)

So, there's Arnold Jones, held up by all these hands, <u>flopping</u> and <u>kicking</u> and <u>shrieking</u> like some poor Aztec human sacrifice about to be tossed off a pyramid. (p. 17)

The phantom Samaritan <u>stuck the book between his teeth</u>, <u>crouched down</u>, <u>hoisted Arnold Jones's limp carcass over his shoulder</u>, and <u>hauled him out of there like a sack of flour</u>. (p. 19)

So, <u>from the dump</u>, <u>from the creek</u>, <u>from the tracks</u>, <u>from Red Hill</u>—in ran the Pickwell kids for dinner, all ten of them. (p. 20)

He would need <u>the touch of a surgeon</u>, <u>the alertness of an owl</u>, <u>the cunning of three foxes</u>, and <u>the foresight of a grand master in chess</u>. (p. 73)

She was holding one of the homemade confetti scraps, gaping at it. Then she was <u>scrambling across the sidewalk</u>, <u>the street</u>, <u>shoving people's legs aside</u>, <u>grabbing more scraps</u>, <u>crying out</u>, "Oh no! . . . Oh *no!*" And then she was running. (p. 75)

He laid the new ball in the palm, pressed glove and ball together, and the glove <u>remembered</u> and <u>gave way</u> and <u>made a pocket for the ball</u>. (p. 114)

When just two items are joined as grammatically equal elements, they too are parallel:

<u>Inside his house</u>, a kid gets one name, but <u>on the other side of the door</u>, it's whatever the rest of the world wants to call him. (p. 53)

<u>She didn't like</u> this boy bringing the vacant lot into her kitchen, and <u>she didn't like</u> how it fit his mouth. (p. 55, referring to Maniac's use of "trash talk")

Then the music ended, and Jeffrey went right on screaming, <u>his face bright red by now</u>, <u>his neck bulging</u>. (p. 6)

After polishing off the Krimpets, Maniac did the last thing anybody expected: he lay down and took a nap right there on the table, <u>the knot hanging above him like a small hairy planet</u>, <u>the mob buzzing all around him</u>. (p. 72; "Lay down" and "took a nap" would technically qualify as parallelism with two elements, but the grammar isn't entirely identical and the rhetorical effect is minimal.)

So they went outside and crossed the creek and tramped the woods until they came to a fine and proper evergreen, and there, <u>their footsteps muffled by the carpet of pine needles,</u> <u>their every breath and whispered word arrayed in frosty white,</u> they trimmed their second tree. (p. 111)

Traditionally, only three or more "like" items have been considered examples of parallelism. Why? Perhaps because joining two simple items like *cats* and *dogs* hardly seems stylistically effective enough to be considered an example of parallelism. The term *parallelism* describes a rhetorical device designed to have a particular effect upon readers, often through content as well as structure, and this effect is sometimes accomplished with only two "like" items. The parallel structure emphasizes the content.

A8 comma uses relating to modifiers and parallelism

It may seem strange to include major uses of the comma along with modifying phrases and parallelism, but commas are used most frequently with those kinds of constructions—especially if we stretch the concept of parallel constructions to include any grammatical elements that are compounded, even when there are only two of them and even when (in the case of conjoined simple sentences, for instance) their internal structures may differ noticeably.

The following examples of set-off modifiers are almost all taken from the student writing done in Grammar in Teaching Writing, a primarily undergraduate course at Western Michigan University that also enrolls a few graduate students. Most of these students claimed that they seldom used the set-off adjectival constructions until they took this course.

While Jeff Anderson (inspired by Carroll and Wilson, 1993) was teaching four major uses of the comma to his sixth graders, I was teaching essentially the same four uses to my college students. In the following sections I have borrowed Jeff's simpler terms, and the first three of his diagrams (Anderson, 2005, p. 167).

A8-a opener

A comma is used after an introductory adverbial clause, any long introductory phrase, and any short phrase after which you want the reader to pause noticeably. In addition, a comma goes after certain kinds of introductory words: the name of someone being addressed; words like *well* and *yes*, which bear no grammatical relationship to the rest of the sentence;

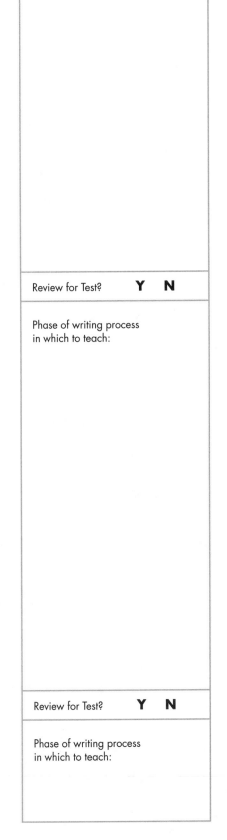

Review for Test?   **Y**   **N**

Phase of writing process in which to teach:

Review for Test?   **Y**   **N**

Phase of writing process in which to teach:

and words and phrases like *however, nevertheless, of course,* and *for example.*

Use a comma to set off an **opener.**

Opener, `sentence` .

Anxious, I waited for Rollie's head to appear above the water.

Long ago, I was taught this way, but they teach something different today.

Although clothed in sunshine and whitecaps, she obviously wasn't an angel.

Three surgeries and eight months later, I found myself enrolled in the blind rehabilitation program at Western.

Raving about Jenny's achievement, I didn't even hear my mother ask, "Where is she now?"

Frustrated and discouraged, but still going strong, I find my purpose in life is to teach them all.

Finally, she was old enough to go to school.

"Right now, please get out your workbooks and do pages 6 and 7."

Yes, it is true, I was one hour twenty-three minutes and thirty-nine seconds late for school this morning, but please let me explain.

As I held my breath, shifting my eyes from one child to the next, praying these kids would not devour me the very first day, they poured into the classroom, chattering and wrestling with one another.

Casey, I wouldn't do that if I were you.

Well, Marvin, I can't really say.

Oops, I didn't see the cat.

Cheri, that's okay.

However, these were just drafts of their writing and not final products.

For example, there isn't one good movie theater in town.

A8-b interrupter

Any kind of interrupting, nonessential element requires commas around it. Such elements include the kinds of introductory words and phrases mentioned under A8-a, "Opener," when they are used somewhere in the middle of the sentence: *well, yes, however, of course*, and similar examples.

Use **two** commas to set off an *interrupter*.

Sent, *Interrupter,* ence .

The sunlight, showing through the drifting clouds, played hide and seek with us.

He left the house swiftly, in the night, never to return.

An older man, knobby-kneed and trim, clips on his harness.

Sydney, young and cute, ran across the room.

My husband's eyes, those eyes our daughters have, were a different shade of blue.

He came into our lives in an unusual way, this stranger, this boy of Summer who would change the lives of my 5-year-olds.

Sunday suddenly felt like a heavy weight, a pile of bricks that someone had placed on my shoulders, crushing me little by little until I crumbled into a mound of human flesh.

We still remember the way you sat, red pen in your hand, correcting our essays in the courageous attempt to learn us all real good. ("Learn us all real good" is used ironically, to make a point.)

I love you, Harley Davidson, with all my heart.

I can't really say, James, which of these books you'd like best; they're both great.

That, of course, is when our trip was scheduled.

"Your dirty boots," she muttered, "don't belong in the living room."

Don't panic, I thought, don't panic.

This, the book said, was the kind of thing that could happen on Costa Rican rivers in the rainy season.

A8-c closer

Any final nonessential element requires a comma before it. Such elements include the kinds of introductory words and phrases mentioned under "Opener" when they are used somewhere at the end the sentence: *well, yes, however, of course*, and similar examples.

Use a comma to set off a ***closer.***

Sentence, ***closer.***

I nourish it who can nourish nothing, <u>love's slipshod watchman</u>.
(Y. Yevtushenko, "Colours")

These activities are fun because there are many possibilities, <u>many of which are funny</u>.

I was so shocked I couldn't even look in the direction where the noise came from, <u>behind the closed door</u>.

In the past, I have always been told I was an exceptional writer, <u>seldom making any significant grammatical mistakes</u>.

I'm amazed at what some of these kids are doing with their writing, <u>especially Dean</u>.

Reading all these papers is tiring, <u>unfortunately</u>.

Like a slow-motion side show, I see Jenny crumpled up at the bottom of the stairs, <u>body limp</u>, <u>sobbing silently</u>.

Our hurried lifestyle soon takes over, <u>plunging us forever into chaos</u>.

"I'm not doing well," <u>he said</u>.

I'm just sorry, <u>okay</u>?

You can go with me to Disney World, <u>yes</u>.

I appreciate your help, <u>Mr. Evans</u>.

A8-d series separator

Whether or not we lump compound and parallel items into a single category with respect to comma use, they are almost always separated by a comma (though a coordinator is expected as well between two simple sentences).

Use a comma to separate compound items

item , ***item***

and to separate items in a series.

item , ***item*** , ***item***

In the following examples, the compounded or parallel items have not been underlined, but the comma use should be clear.

I always wanted to be somebody, but I should have been more specific.

—Lily Tomlin

I don't know the key to success, but the key to failure is trying to please everybody.

—Bill Cosby

Not everything that can be counted counts, and not everything that counts can be counted.

—Albert Einstein

In Germany they came first for the Communists, and I didn't speak up because I wasn't a Communist. Then they came for the Jews, and I didn't speak up because I wasn't a Jew. Then they came for the trade unionists, and I didn't speak up because I wasn't a trade unionist. Then they came for the Catholics, and I didn't speak up because I was a Protestant. Then they came for me, and by that time no one was left to speak up.

—Martin Niemoeller, German Lutheran pastor

It is not a tax bill, but a tax relief bill, providing relief not for the needy but for the greedy.

—Margaret Mead

You either have to be first, best, or different.

—Loretta Lynn

Some men are born great, some achieve greatness, and some hire public-relations writers.

—Daniel Boorstin

The terrible, dreaded order comes in the form of a telegram. There is no choice, no hope, and no escape.

—Meredith MacMillan, in Noden's *Image Grammar*

Between what can be seen and what must be feared, between what lives and what never dies, between the light of truth and the darkness of evil, lies the future of terror.

—United Artists, *The Twilight Zone*

Like every great river and every great sea, the moon belongs to none and belongs to all. It still holds the key to madness, still controls the tides that lap on shore everywhere, still guards the lovers that kiss in every land under no banner but the sky.

—Scott Elledge

Whither thou goest, I will go; and where thou lodgest, I will lodge; thy people shall be my people, and thy God, my God.

—The Bible, Ruth 1:16

The Sentence

Structure, Organization, Punctuation—and More

Addressing organization (transitions), sentence fluency, and editing conventions of subject-verb agreement and punctuation

---

What practical value is there in understanding and being able to identify subjects and verbs? First, it sets the stage for making verbs agree with their subjects, an editing skill that is often taught. Second, it enables us to identify clauses and then apply conventions, or "rules," for how to separate or join them. To that end, this section addresses both the basic parts of a sentence and these related editing skills.

Understanding the basic functions of the parts of a sentence is crucial. Structural linguists have identified four functional elements within a sentence:

Nominal: Any word or group of words functioning the way a noun does.

Verbal: Any word or group of words functioning the way a verb does, as a predicate.

Adjectival: Any word or group of words functioning the way an adjective does.

Adverbial: Any word or group of words functioning the way an adverb does.

Note that this concept of "verbal" differs from how the term is used in traditional grammars. These broad categories, explained in subsequent sections, keep our focus on the *functions* of grammatical elements rather than on labeling each and every word in a sentence. This, in turn, makes it easier to focus on how sentences can be enriched to add detail, voice, and style.

Any group of words functioning together in the same way—nominal, verbal, adjectival, or adverbial—can be called a *construction*, but how the construction functions within the sentence is more important for writers than the construction's internal make-up.

The following grammatical concepts and terms will be discussed in this section in the order listed, along with the related editing issues:

How a construction functions within the sentence is more important for writers than the construction's internal make-up.

- Subject and predicate: nominal + verbal
  - Nominal as subject (noun, noun phrase, pronoun)
  - Verbal as predicate (main verb, auxiliary verb, verb phrase)
  - Subject-verb agreement
  - Independent clauses; simple and compound sentences
  - Joining independent clauses
  - Avoiding run-on and comma-splice sentences and ineffective fragments
- Modifying functions: adjectival and adverbial (a brief review)
- Beyond the simple: subordinating (dependent) clauses and complex sentences

Five of the traditional eight parts of speech are mentioned in this list; three others—coordinating conjunctions, subordinating conjunctions, and prepositions—are implicit. (The interjection is not really a part of speech, but a function that almost any word or group of words can perform.)

To reiterate: This section focuses primarily on the function of words and groups of words, not on their forms. By becoming familiar with these concepts and terms (and a very few more), plus examples, teachers and students can talk about grammatical options, style, and conventions with relative ease.

B1 subject and predicate

The two basic parts of a sentence, any sentence, are the *subject* and the *predicate*. *Sentence* here is a technical grammatical term; it doesn't just mean whatever starts with a capital and ends with a period. Often, what we, our students, and professional writers punctuate as a sentence is effective in context, even though not grammatically complete. But a *grammatically complete sentence* means, minimally, a subject-predicate unit. The subject designates someone or something, and the predicate tells about it. The subject consists solely of a nominal, which may be as simple as a single word: a *noun* or *pronoun*. At its simplest, the predicate, too, may be a single word: a *verb*. Here are sentences that consist of just a noun and a verb:

Children dream.	Hope endures.
Elephants trudge.	Butter melts.
Storms threaten.	Garbage stinks.
Computers quit.	Physics mystifies.
Currents swirled.	Mathematics beckons.
Rafts overturned.	Marnie sang.
People jumped.	Roger chuckled.
Water rippled.	Reiko shuddered.

Since two-word sentences seldom occur in writing, these sentences may sound a bit odd. Furthermore, you may have noticed that many of the example subjects—*children, elephants, storms, computers, currents, rafts*—are plural, which means they indicate more than one. When we use most common nouns in the singular form, we would have to add a pointing word, at a minimum:

<u>The</u> child dreams.

<u>An</u> elephant trudges.

<u>The</u> computer quit.

<u>A</u> current swirled.

These sentences, too, are rather basic and would not often occur in writing. Indeed, most predicates consist of more than just a verb. Certain linguists, in fact, use the term *verbal* to refer to the verb phrase plus anything that is required or optional after it. (In traditional grammar, the term *verbal* is applied to verb forms when they are *not* working as verbs!)

The following diagram shows the basic parts of a sentence: a subject and a predicate. Predicates may be expanded in various ways, and such predicates will be included in some of our examples, typically without comment. In a grammar for writers and teachers of writers, there is little need to focus on the other parts of the predicate, though they'll be briefly mentioned later.

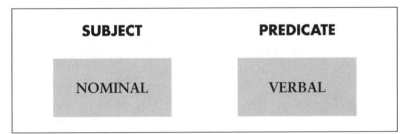

SUBJECT   PREDICATE

NOMINAL   VERBAL

B2   nominal in the subject function

At its most basic, a nominal may function as the subject of a verb or as an object of some kind. The subject function is the most crucial—all sentences must have a subject—and that is what's discussed here.

B2-a   noun

Unmodified single-word nouns and pronouns are the simplest kind of subject a sentence can have. A *noun* designates someone or something: *child*,

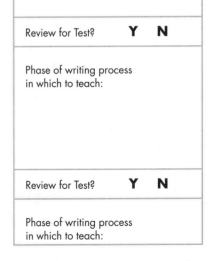

elephant, storm, computer, current, raft, people, water, hope, butter, garbage, physics, mathematics, Marnie, Roger, Reiko.

A noun usually is made plural or possessive by adding an ending: for example, *child/children, child's/children's; elephant/elephant's, elephants/elephants'; raft/rafts, raft's/rafts'; mathematics'* difficulty (the difficulty of mathematics). Names like *Roger* can be made possessive, as in *Roger's home.* Less obviously, they can be made plural in certain contexts: *there are two Rogers in our class.* Most *common* (and therefore uncapitalized) *nouns,* in fact, can be both singular and plural. Most kinds of nouns can take *the* in front of them: <u>*the*</u> child, <u>*the*</u> elephants, <u>*the*</u> computer, <u>*the*</u> rafts, <u>*the*</u> people, <u>*the*</u> water, <u>*the*</u> hope, <u>*the*</u> garbage. But this "test" for a potential noun—seeing if *the* can be put in front of the word, out of context— doesn't work for all nouns: We wouldn't ordinarily say <u>*the*</u> Marnie, <u>*the*</u> Roger, or <u>*the*</u> Reiko. *Proper nouns,* the names of specific persons, places, or things, are capitalized. Many proper nouns that aren't personal names take *the* before them: <u>*the*</u> United States, <u>*the*</u> Grand Canyon, <u>*the*</u> Department of Justice, <u>*the*</u> University of Ohio, <u>*the*</u> SAT, and so on.

Nouns as subjects have been illustrated in the previous set of sentences, where they were labeled by the more inclusive term *nominal.* Again, a *nominal* is any word or group of words that functions like a noun.

B2-b noun phrase

A noun is a single word; a *noun phrase* is a noun plus any words describing it. In the following examples, the noun phrases are underlined; all function as subjects of their sentences:

<u>The excited *children*</u> dreamed.   <u>Heated *butter*</u> melts.
<u>All the *computers* in our lab</u> quit.   <u>My *Uncle Joe*</u> left.
<u>The dangerous, muddy *currents*</u> swirled. <u>The *raft* we were in</u> capsized.
<u>His stalled *car*</u> balked.   <u>Untapped *energy*</u> exists.

Each phrase has a head noun, indicated in italic type. Like single nouns, noun phrases are nominals.

Identifying nominals

We can tell that a word or group of words is a nominal if we can replace it with a placeholder—*someone (some ones)* or *something (some things).* This is true for any nominal in a sentence, not just one functioning as the subject.

Phase of writing process
in which to teach:

B2-c pronoun

The pronoun is another kind of nominal. Pronouns can "take the place of" or "stand for" a noun or noun phrase (hence the term *pro-noun*, meaning "for a noun"). Unlike nouns, pronouns are few in number. Pronouns include words like *I, you, he, she, it, we, they*, and their related forms (*me, my; your, yours; him, his; her, hers; its; them, their, theirs*). These *personal pronouns* refer to someone or something that has already been identified, either in the same sentence (or a previous one) or by the nonverbal context.

Teachers of writing don't necessarily need to know the names for the other subcategories of pronouns, but the names are useful in organizing the examples. The four *demonstrative* pronouns—*this, these, that*, and *those*—can be used instead of a noun to designate something identified or identifiable in the verbal or nonverbal context: *I want this book you just handed me, not those books on the shelf.* On the other hand, *indefinite pronouns* like *someone, something, anyone, anybody, no one, nobody, everyone*, and *everybody* are sometimes used when there is no specific noun for them to refer to; they are broad cover terms. Pronouns used to question are called *interrogative pronouns*: *what, who, which*, and sometimes *whose* or *whom*, as in *who's there?* These *WH-word pronouns*, as they are often called, have different names when they function in other ways.

The words mentioned as demonstratives and interrogatives do not always fill a nominal slot, but when they do, they are—by definition—pronouns. Or to put it the other way, by definition a pronoun is a certain kind of nominal; the same word functioning differently is not a pronoun. Here are examples of pronouns:

He knows.

That isn't true.

Everyone is important.

Nobody knows what to do.

What happened?

In the second example, the pronoun *that* doesn't necessarily refer to a single noun. Often, the pronouns *it, this*, and *that* are used more generally, to refer to an entire statement or question previously made or implied. For example: *Who started the fight? Charlie didn't do it; that isn't true.* Traditional grammar handbooks urge students not to use pronouns to refer to more than a single noun, but the use of a pronoun to refer to a whole phrase or sentence is often clear and frequently found in published writing.

B3 verbal

In addition to the subject, the only required part of a sentence is a predicate—a *verbal*, as defined by certain linguists—and the only required part of the predicate/verbal is a verb.

B3-a verb

Traditionally a *verb* is said to show action or express a state of being, though obviously this definition is vague, requiring examples and clarification. In the previous sentences where nouns were illustrated (B2-a), the other word in each sentence is a verb. Additional examples are underlined in the following sentences. To illustrate a greater range of verbs than before, I have included other words after them, without explanation as to how these other words are functioning.

> The UFO <u>hovered</u> above us. I <u>am</u> fully alive.
> Samantha <u>chortled</u> with glee. Frankenstein <u>isn't</u> my favorite monster.
> Carlos <u>has</u> a Jaguar. Four chemical elements <u>are</u> basic.

Out of context, a word has the potential to be a verb if it has both a present and a past tense (as well as certain other forms, illustrated elsewhere):

> hover/hovered has/had
> chortle/chortled have/had
> go/went am/was
> sleep/slept is/was
> sing/sang are/were
> become/became

Many students of the language seem to have difficulty recognizing the verb in a sentence when it is one of the forms of *to be*: *am, is, are, was, were,* in particular. That's why these common verb forms were illustrated in the previous set. Overall, verbs express doing, having, being, or becoming. The key to identifying a verb, though, is how it works in a sentence.

B3-b main verb, auxiliary verb, and verb phrase

A verb is called a *main verb* if one or more auxiliary verbs come before it. Together, they function as a unit, a *verb phrase*. (These are the terms commonly used in traditional schoolroom grammar.) In the examples below, the auxiliary verbs are underlined and the main verbs are italicized.

Gilgamesh <u>was</u> *leaving*.

Marguerite <u>has</u> *left* the stage.

He <u>might have</u> *gone* to get her.

Cinderella <u>should be</u> *dancing* soon.

Everyone <u>should have</u> *arrived* by six o'clock.

Rolland <u>is</u> *fishing* right from the dock.

He <u>has</u> *caught* twenty fish already.

The fish <u>have been</u> *rolled* in pancake mix.

In just a few minutes, we <u>will be</u> *eating* fried blue gills.

Knowing the auxiliary verbs and seeing how they combine is useful in identifying the verb phrase in a sentence. If more than one auxiliary is used, the elements of the verb phrase occur in this order:

(modal) + (a form of *have*) + (a form of *be*) + main verb

Linguists use parentheses to indicate optional elements. A verb never requires an auxiliary, so the auxiliaries are shown as options, in parentheses. Following is a list of the auxiliaries in English:

MODAL	FORMS OF *HAVE*	FORMS OF *TO BE*
can	have	be
could	has	am
will	had	is
would	having	are
shall		was
should		were
may		been
might		being
must		

Modals qualify a verb somehow. Certain two-word combinations, particularly *used to*, *ought to*, and *supposed to*, sometimes work as modals within sentences: *Sheila <u>used to</u> worry*; *Carmalita <u>ought to</u> be leaving*; *Zack is <u>supposed to</u> clock the swimmers*. The main verbs are *worry*, *leaving*, and *clock*, respectively.

If you experiment with using auxiliaries before a main verb, you'll soon discover that when you have two or more auxiliaries, there are strict limits as to what form can be used for every auxiliary after the first, and for the main verb. The example sentences above cover most of the possibilities.

Review for Test?   **Y   N**

Phase of writing process
in which to teach:

B4   subject-verb agreement

In theory, subject-verb agreement is a big deal: We must make subjects and verbs agree or else appear uneducated. But that applies mostly to basic subject-verb agreement.

   The issue of agreement between subjects and verbs arises only with present-tense verbs. The conventional standard calls for a teeter-totter relationship between subjects and verbs. Most nouns take an *-s* or *-es* to make them plural, though not all do. When the subject is plural, the verb has no *-s* or *-es* ending:

   The giants tiptoe quietly through the garden.

   The new cars still use too much gasoline.

   Those boxes clutter my garage.

   The children run circles around the rest of us.

   My friends box every Saturday night.

On the other hand, when the subject is singular, a regular verb will take *-s* or *-es* to agree with its subject:

   The giant tiptoes quietly through the garden.

   The new car still uses too much gasoline.

   This box clutters my garage.

   The child runs circles around the rest of us.

   Calvin boxes every Saturday night.

The verb *to be* has special forms: *am, is,* and *are* for the present tense, *was* and *were* for the past tense. The verb *to have* includes *have* and *has* as present tense forms, *had* for the past tense. For some speakers and writers, these forms generate special issues with agreement; see Section D1 comparing informal and formal variants of language.

So, what are the real difficulties with subject-verb agreement that plague most of us as writers and teachers? Following are some situations and examples.

B4-a when two compound subjects are joined

Except in instances when a compound subject is thought of as a single unit, as in *The bed and breakfast [a place to stay] was cozy*, compound subjects joined by *and* are considered plural and take the verb form that goes with plural subjects. The correlative conjunction pair *both . . . and* functions the same way.

The pit and the pendulum <u>are</u> both to be avoided.

Both the motorcycle and the speedboat <u>belong</u> to Josh.

Singular subjects joined by *or* take the verb form that goes with singular nouns. The pair of correlative conjunctions *either . . . or* and *neither . . . nor* work the same way.

The dog *or* the cat <u>has</u> scattered all the food.

Either Carmen *or* Melissa <u>is</u> helping with the work.

Neither the plumber *nor* the electrician <u>wants</u> to do the work.

In other words, when two singular subjects are joined by *or*, the subject is treated as if it is singular. But what if the word *or* joins a singular subject with a plural subject? In that case, the verb is made to agree with the nearer noun.

This river or at least the nearby streams <u>flood</u> every year.

Either the ants *or* the carpenter <u>dances</u> every year.

Neither the bricklayer *nor* the concrete pourers <u>are</u> ready.

B4-b when a prepositional phrase or other construction separates the subject and verb

In the following examples, it helps to identify the verb, identify the subject by temporarily removing the intervening material, and then check to be sure that the verb agrees grammatically with the subject.

B4 subject-verb agreement   **103**

The <u>clusters</u> of students standing apart from the crowd <u>are</u> groups from our school.

It's nearly two o'clock when the <u>secretaries</u> in that office finally <u>get</u> to take a lunch break.

B4-c when the subject and verb are inverted

The following are examples of an inverted subject and verb.

Whether or not to start our vacation early by cutting classes <u>is</u>
<u>the question</u>.
        ↑   ↑
   subject   verb

Putting the question back in "normal" word order can help us see the correct agreement: *The question is whether or not to start our vacation early by cutting classes.* The verb does not agree with *classes*, even though the two words are next to each other in the inverted sentence.

Often, an inverted sentence will begin with an empty *there* that has no relationship to place, or with an empty *it* that refers to no particular noun:

There <u>are</u> four policemen living in our neighborhood. (The "underlying" sentence is "Four policemen are living in our neighborhood," so the verb agrees with *policemen*.)

It <u>is</u> a shame more people don't take advantage of free cultural opportunities. (The underlying subject is the noun clause that "more people don't take advantage of free cultural opportunities.")

B4-d when the subject is an indefinite pronoun

Some of the most common indefinite pronouns are *any, anybody, each, every, everybody, everyone, nobody, no one, none, someone, somebody,* and *some.* All of these indefinite pronouns are singular, though certain ones are most often used in a plural sense. Nevertheless, they take the verb form that goes with singulars:

Not: Everyone in the hall <u>are</u> working on a project. (The meaning is plural, but *everyone* is singular in form.)

But: Everyone in the hall <u>is</u> working on a project.

The Sentence

Not: Each <u>are</u> responsible for their own lunchboxes.

Correct but awkward: Each <u>is</u> responsible for his or her lunchbox.

Correct and better: All <u>are</u> responsible for their own lunchboxes.

There are really two issues here: the verb form, and what pronoun or pronouns to use. The two issues occur together so often that sometimes it is just better to restructure the sentence with a different indefinite pronoun—typically a plural one—as the subject. For more on pronoun agreement, see Section C2-d.

There are so many rules for making verbs agree with specific kinds of subjects that a complete treatment of subject-verb agreement is beyond the scope of this section. For simple but more complete coverage, you might try Douglas Cazort's *Under the Grammar Hammer* (1997). For more complete and more complex coverage, try Diana Hacker's *A Writer's Reference* (2003), which is designed for college students. (Standardized tests like the ACT and the SAT usually do have some questions on the finer points of subject-verb agreement.)

B5 independent clause

An *independent clause* is simply a subject-predicate unit that can stand by itself as a grammatically complete sentence. Thus "independent clause" and "simple sentence" are synonymous. Particularly when there is more than one clause in a sentence, an independent clause is often referred to as a *main clause*.

A *punctuated sentence*—what occurs between the initial capital and the final period—may include more than one independent clause. These independent clauses may be joined by a comma plus a *coordinating conjunction*:

The currents swirled <u>and</u> the raft capsized.

Rollie leaped <u>but</u> Connie fell.

The other common coordinating conjunctions are *or, so, yet,* and sometimes *for* or *nor.* Most of these coordinators may also be used to conjoin other grammatical elements of the same kind—that is, grammatically parallel elements.

B5-a joining and separating independent clauses (simple sentences)

A *simple sentence* is merely one independent (main) clause, with no dependent clauses. There are five basic ways of relating simple sentences:

Review for Test?   **Y**   **N**

Phase of writing process in which to teach:

Review for Test?   **Y**   **N**

Phase of writing process in which to teach:

- With a period, which obliterates any relationship, if indeed there is one:

Daryl scored the winning touchdown. Afterwards the team went out to celebrate together.

- With a comma plus a coordinating conjunction (*and, but, or, so, yet, for, nor*):

Daryl scored the winning touchdown, <u>and</u> his teammates carried him off the field on their shoulders.

Daryl scored the winning touchdown, <u>but</u> he didn't take credit for winning the game.

- With a colon, when the first simple sentence serves as a "trumpet" introducing the second one:

It was amazing<u>:</u> Even some members of the losing team cheered the winners.

- With a semicolon, which both separates and relates (think of the top part as being a period, to separate, and the bottom part as being a comma, to relate):

The cheerleaders jumped and shouted<u>;</u> the crowd roared.

- With a semicolon plus a conjunctive adverb:

Daryl tried to avoid the media<u>; however,</u> three reporters immediately stuck their microphones in his face.

Daryl tried to avoid the media; three reporters, <u>however,</u> immediately stuck their microphones in his face.

The emphasized connectors in these last sentences are conjunctive adverbs: They join, like coordinating conjunctions, but they and the clauses they introduce typically have an adverbial sense. Some conjunctive adverbs need to be set off by a comma or commas; others don't. By reading a sentence aloud, you can usually tell whether the conjunctive adverb needs to be set off.

How have conjunctive adverbs gotten their name? Well, they join together—that is, conjoin—two simple sentences, but they also have an adverbial meaning, and indeed they all can work as adverbials within a sentence.

WORDS AND PHRASES THAT COMMONLY SERVE AS CONJUNCTIVE ADVERBS (or as regular adverbials)

also	accordingly	as a result
besides	consequently	for example
hence	furthermore	for instance

indeed	however	in fact
instead	meanwhile	of course
then	moreover	on the other hand
thus	nevertheless	
	therefore	

It surprises many people to learn that when the word *then* joins two simple sentences, it is considered a conjunctive adverb and therefore the rule calls for it to be preceded by a semicolon, not a comma. The same is true of *thus*, as well as all the other connecting words and phrases in the preceding list.

B5-b avoiding run-on or comma-splice sentences and ineffective fragments

A *run-on sentence* contains two (or more) independent clauses with no joining word or punctuation between them:

He ran and ran he just couldn't help it.

A *comma-splice sentence* contains two (or more) independent clauses joined with just a comma—no conjoining word like *and* or *but*:

He ran and ran, he just couldn't help it.

Sometimes the best way to solve a comma splice is simply to subordinate one of the independent clauses to the other:

                                                         where
Margola drifted away from her parents and into the jungle, ~~there~~ she played happily for five hours.

When
↑ Margola got lonesome, then she tried to find the path she had followed.

In the last example, the sentence probably sounds better when the word *then* is omitted.

Sometimes a comma-splice sentence can be effective; both Weaver (1996) and Schuster (2003) include discussions that draw upon Brosnahan (1976). However, comma-splice sentences are not widely accepted or often used in most published writing.

A *fragment* is grammatically less than a complete sentence (not a subject-plus-complete-verb unit). Fragments can be effective or ineffective, depending partly on the context. Some fragments do not work very well when punctuated as a complete sentence. For example:

Review for Test?   **Y**   **N**

Phase of writing process in which to teach:

<u>What if.</u> He didn't do it.

<u>What he did.</u> <u>Was throw the baseball fast and hard.</u>

We went boating and waterskiing. <u>And exhausted.</u>

Ricky suffers from arachnophobia. <u>A fear of spiders.</u>

<u>Although the paramedics knew it was too late.</u> They gave him CPR anyway.

She wondered what to do next. <u>Being that she had completed all her work.</u>

Jack offered to lift the heavy box. <u>Which didn't bother me a bit.</u>

Some fragments that occur after what they describe need to be attached to the preceding sentence. Here's just one example:

The figure skater stood tall and confident. <u>Waiting for his points.</u> $\longrightarrow$

The figure skater stood tall and confident, waiting for his points.

However, we would not simply join the fragment *being that she had completed all her work* to the preceding sentence in the earlier example; "standard" usage calls for *since* instead of *being that*: *She wondered what to do next, <u>since</u> she had completed all her work.*

Many fragments do not need to be attached to what came before; they are effective as is, often to emphasize a point or respond to a question. Smart teachers will help students distinguish between effective and ineffective fragments in their writing, and then, when appropriate, remind them that all fragments are considered wrong on standardized multiple-choice tests.

Here are some examples of effective fragments:

All the guy asked for was five dollars. <u>A measly five bucks.</u>

The leader of the gang lunged toward me. <u>Time to move. NOW!</u>

<u>What?</u>

<u>Who, me?</u>

I won the lottery? <u>Impossible. Totally and utterly impossible.</u>

Effective fragments occur in context, usually after a sentence that makes their meaning perfectly clear. (What contexts might have come before the fragments *What?* and *Who, me?*)

Sometimes a fragment is a subordinate clause that, regardless of its location, can simply be added to the main sentence, with a comma if/as appropriate:

Although the paramedics knew it was too late, they gave him CPR anyway.

Jack offered to lift the heavy box, which didn't bother me a bit.

Published writers these days, particularly writers of fiction and creative nonfiction, sometimes present a clause like *which didn't bother me a bit* as a fragment, but conservative usage would have us attach the clause to the preceding sentence. For other examples of effective fragments, see Section D4-d.

It is important to help students *in the context of writing meaningful paragraphs and pieces* learn to choose conjoining, subordinating, and other connecting words and phrases appropriate to the meaning and the transitional moves they want to make.

B6 modifying functions: adjectival and adverbial

Adjectival and adverbial modifiers are discussed in Section A, so their functions are simply defined and illustrated here.

B6-a adjectival

An *adjectival* may consist of an *adjective* or other single word or a group of words, including an entire subordinate clause (subject-predicate unit). An adjectival functions to modify a noun.

The overconfident visiting team lost.

The visiting team, which was overconfident, lost.

Overconfident, the visiting team lost.

The home team won.

Eager fans mobbed the players.

Fans, who were eager to congratulate the players, streamed onto the floor.

Fans, eager to congratulate the players, streamed onto the floor.

Eager to congratulate the players, fans streamed onto the floor.

Fans streamed onto the floor, eager to congratulate the players.

The clauses in the above sentences can be reduced to a single word or phrase (a group of words that does not consist of a subject-verb unit). Following are more examples:

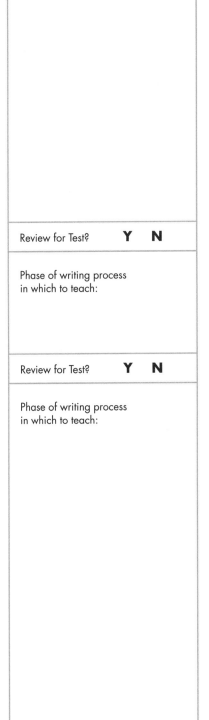

Review for Test?   **Y   N**

Phase of writing process
in which to teach:

Review for Test?   **Y   N**

Phase of writing process
in which to teach:

The <u>barn</u> door creaked.

The door <u>to the barn</u> creaked.

The <u>barn</u> door, <u>which was loose on its hinges</u>, creaked.

<u>Loose on its hinges</u>, the barn door creaked.

And here's another set with a different subject and verb:

The <u>distant</u> lightning crackled.

The <u>distant</u> lightning, <u>which was accompanied by gentle thunder</u>, crackled.

The <u>distant</u> lightning crackled, <u>accompanied by gentle thunder</u>.

You might consider whether *accompanied by gentle thunder* sounds as good in other locations or not, and why.

Technically *the* is an adjectival, but not an adjective: it is a *determiner*. For more examples, see Section A2.

B6-b adverbial

An *adverbial* may consist of an *adverb* or other single word or a group of words, including an entire subordinate clause (subject-predicate unit). An adverbial functions to modify a verb or the entire main clause. Traditionally, an adverb is said to tell *how* (in what manner); *how long* or *how far* (to what extent); or *where, when,* or *why* with respect to the action. In what position do the adverbials in the following examples sound best?

The home team won <u>easily</u> [how].

The barn door creaked <u>loudly</u> [how] <u>in protest</u> [how or why (in order to protest)].

<u>In protest</u> [how or why], the barn door creaked <u>loudly</u> [how].

The distant lightning cracked <u>repeatedly</u> [how].

<u>Repeatedly</u> [how], the distant lightning crackled.

The distant lightning crackled <u>like breaking glass</u> [how] <u>in the distance</u> [where].

<u>In the distance</u> [where], the distant lightning crackled <u>like breaking glass</u> [how].

The distant lightning crackled <u>for hours</u> [how long].

<u>For hours</u> [how long] the distant lightning crackled.

We gazed <u>forever</u> [how long] at the distant lightning <u>because it was so beautiful</u> [why].

When they emerged [when], they saw the lightning crackling in the distance [where].

Review for Test?   Y   N

B7 the predicate expanded

Phase of writing process in which to teach:

Grammatically speaking, the verb is the strongest element in a sentence: It controls what kind of construction, if any, will occur after it in the predicate. ("The subject does what the predicate says," according to the old TV program *Schoolhouse Rock*). The preceding sections have mostly illustrated verbs that can occur with nothing after them in the predicate. Here is a sampling:

Children dream.   Hope endures.
Computers quit.   People jumped.

Such verbs are called *intransitive*, because they do not carry action over to anything (from Latin: *in* = not, *trans* = across, *it* = to go). Verbs are also intransitive when they are followed by just an optional adverbial:

Children dream often.   Hope endures forever.
Children dream in color.   Hope endures despite everything.
Computers quit daily.   People jumped quickly.
Computers quit every day.   People jumped into the raging current.
The UFO hovered above us.   Samantha chortled with glee.
He might have gone to get her.   Eager fans streamed onto the floor.

In each case the adverbial relates to the action but is not required.

In other instances, though, the verb may have, or even require, a nominal after it:

Children dream many things.   The home team won the game.
The waiters quit their jobs.   The fans mobbed the players.
He has caught twenty fish.   The lightning hit our maple tree.
Junie's question required an answer. The lightning frightened Sandy.

Some of these verbs can also be intransitive, as in previous examples, but *caught, required, mobbed,* and *frightened* seem to require a nominal after them. Such nominals are said to "receive the action of the verb." When a nominal performs that function, it is called a *direct object* of the verb. The verb is said to be *transitive* when it carries action across ("trans") from the subject to the direct object.

For the curious: An *indirect object* may occur after the verb and before the direct object. An *indirect object* tells to or for whom (or what) something else is given, said, or done. For example: *Jennifer gave her mother a gift*. The nominal *a gift* is the direct object, telling what Jennifer gave. *Her mother* is the indirect object, telling to whom the gift was given. Or take this sentence: *Harry told Hermione the truth*. In this case, Hermione told *the truth* (direct object) to Harry (indirect object). Finally, consider *Jamal did the town a good deed*. What is the direct object? The indirect object? A sentence never has an indirect object unless it is followed by a direct object. To determine if a nominal is working as an indirect object, see if it can be converted into a prepositional phrase after the direct object: *Jennifer gave a gift to her mother*; *Harry told the truth to Hermione*; *Jamal did a good deed for the town*. (See Section A3 for a list of common prepositions and for the basic functions of the prepositional phrase.) Other nominal functions may follow a direct object, but rarely.

Much more common is a nominal right after a so-called linking verb (see below); it is said to "refer back" to the subject. It usually categorizes the subject (names a category into which the subject noun fits) or else identifies the subject nominal:

> Chrysanthemums are <u>flowers</u>.
> Some government officials are <u>terrorists</u>.
> Horatio became <u>a hero</u>.
> He remained <u>a crime fighter</u>.
> That man is <u>Elfie's uncle</u>.
> His store became <u>Sears & Roebuck</u>.
> That mountain is <u>Mt. Shasta</u>.
> This is <u>the beginning of the Amazon</u>.

When a nominal categorizes or identifies the subject, it is called a *predicate nominal*. When a verb links a subject with a predicate nominal, it is called a *linking verb*. Relatively few verbs can function in this way; the major ones are certain forms of *be* and *become*.

A verb may also link a subject with an adjectival that modifies (describes) it:

> That hat is <u>too flowery</u>.   The brownies smelled <u>yummy</u>.
> The crash was <u>terrifying</u>.   They tasted <u>delicious</u>.
> The dough became <u>very stiff</u>.   The car appeared <u>safe</u>.

We can tell that these predicate constructions are adjectival because at least the head adjective could occur before a noun: *<u>flowery</u> hat*, *<u>terrifying</u> crash*, *<u>very stiff</u> dough*, *<u>yummy</u> brownies*, *<u>delicious</u> brownies*, *<u>safe</u> car*. Verbs that link a subject with a predicate adjective are also called linking verbs. They include certain forms of *be* and *become*, plus certain forms of *seem, feel, smell, sound, taste,* and a few others, when used in the same way.

Predicate nominals and adjectivals are also called *complements*, because they in a sense complete the subject nominal—and because some verbs require one of them as part of the verbal phrase. What a person wants to express will determine both the complement and the verb, more or less simultaneously.

B8 beyond the simple: subordinate clauses and the complex sentence

A *simple sentence* consists of just one independent (main) clause and no subordinate clauses. A *compound sentence* has two or more simple sentences. Before concluding this section on the sentence, let me round out the common sentence structures by mentioning the so-called *complex sentence*, which consists of a main clause and one or more subordinate clauses. (The previous sentence is an example.)

The subordinate clause may work adjectivally, to modify a noun or pronoun, or adverbially, to modify a verb (or more often, the entire main clause). The other kind of subordinate clause fills a noun slot in the main sentence. For example:

The stereo <u>that you bought</u> has great sound. (Adjectival, modifying *stereo*.)

Dana bought another one, <u>which doesn't sound as good</u>. (Adjectival, modifying *one*.)

<u>If you buy me a stereo</u>, I'd like to have the same brand and model. (Adverbial, modifying entire main clause.)

I can wait <u>until you can buy Caiden one, too</u>. (Adverbial, modifying verb or main clause.)

I wonder <u>what I'm going to get for my birthday</u>. (Nominal, specifying what I wonder; could be replaced by SOMETHING, which shows it's a nominal.)

<u>Whoever buys me a stereo</u> will get a big "Thank you!" (Nominal, specifying the subject; could be replaced by SOMEONE, which shows it's a nominal.)

The adverbial clauses are introduced by a subordinating conjunction, also called a subordinator: *if* in the first adverbial clause and *until* in the second.

While a sentence with one independent and one dependent clause is technically a complex sentence in traditional grammar, there are many more ways to make a sentence grammatically sophisticated—or, well, complex. Many teachers talk about complex sentences in this more general sense, which can confuse students who have learned the traditional definition of a complex sentence. In our teaching, we might therefore avoid the narrow, technical definition of a complex sentence and just talk about subordinate clauses as needed.

Grammatical Considerations in Choosing the Right Words

Addressing word choices and usage conventions

Several of the conventions of edited American English involve a particular part of speech, typically a verb, pronoun, noun, adjective, or adverb. This section looks at those word choices. (For nonnative speakers of English, the choice of preposition in idiomatic expressions is significant, but beyond the scope of this book.) This section also includes an aside on contractions and a brief discussion of some additional words commonly confused. (Dangling modifiers and the placement of modifiers are both discussed in Section A.)

<table>
<tr><td>Review for Test?</td><td>Y</td><td>N</td></tr>
<tr><td colspan="3">Phase of writing process
in which to teach:</td></tr>
</table>

C1 verbs: consistency of tense

A major concern with verbs is consistency of tense. There are two issues involved: making verbs agree in tense when it's appropriate, not making them agree when it's inappropriate—and, of course, knowing the difference.

> *Inconsistent*: The lead guitarist <u>hung</u> around after the concert, <u>talked</u> with his buddies onstage, and finally <u>comes</u> out to chat with the audience.

These three verbs should be parallel in tense but aren't. The last verb should be changed to past tense, to match the others:

> The lead guitarist <u>hung</u> around after the concert, <u>talked</u> with his buddies onstage, and finally <u>came</u> out to chat with the audience.

This is also an instance of grammatical *parallelism*, as it involves three verb forms in a series.

Inconsistent but correct: The lead guitarist <u>hung</u> around after the concert, <u>talked</u> with his buddies onstage, and finally <u>came</u> out to chat with the audience. He <u>is</u> my best friend.

The first three verbs are in the past tense, so why switch to present tense with *is*? Because the statement about him being my best friend is a generalization: true before, during, and after the events just mentioned. The present tense is used for habitual states or situations. We need to be careful not to insist that students change a present tense verb to past when they are writing about habitual actions, states, or situations within a narrative that is otherwise past tense.

The next sentence is correct for a different reason:

The lead guitarist <u>hung</u> around after the concert and <u>talked</u> with his buddies on stage, finally <u>coming</u> out to chat with the audience.

We no longer have a series of three parallel verb phrases. Instead, the first two parallel verb forms have been joined with *and*, while the third has been made into a participial phrase: *finally <u>coming</u> out to chat with the audience.*

Incidentally, on some standardized tests, the appropriate use of verb tense or form seems to be tested mostly when three or more verb forms occur together in the same sentence or adjacent sentences.

C2 pronoun uses

There are several usage issues regarding pronouns: the use of subject or object form, in general and in subordinate clauses; agreement in number with the noun or pronoun referred to (the *antecedent*); unspecified *they* and *you*; unclear pronoun reference generally; and vague reference with *it*, *this*, *that*, and *which*.

C2-a **use of subject or object form**

The use of *I* or *me* becomes an issue most often with regard to the subject of the sentence. Conventionally, we wouldn't say or write "me went to the concert," because we intuitively know that *me* is not the form to use as subject. However, people who would never say that will sometimes say and write, *Jimmy and me went to the concert.* The trick to avoiding or correcting such a construction is to see how it sounds without mentioning the other person: We'd say *I went to the concert*, so *Jimmy and I went to the concert* is the appropriate wording. Similarly, we can avoid writing

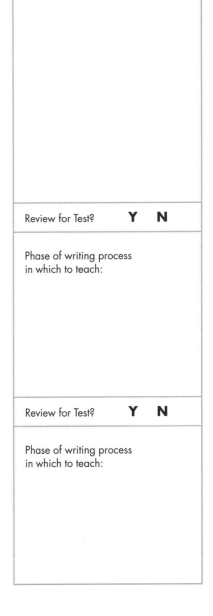

Review for Test?   **Y   N**

Phase of writing process
in which to teach:

Review for Test?   **Y   N**

Phase of writing process
in which to teach:

"<u>him</u> and <u>me</u> went to the concert" by trying just one pronoun at a time as the subject. Neither option sounds right alone, so *he* and *I* are the correct forms.

Many people who have mastered this convention overgeneralize and apply it to situations in which the object form is called for. They say, "please give it to Jimmy and I," rather than the conventional "please give it to Jimmy and me." Again, the way to select the conventional form is to eliminate the other person, namely Jimmy: *Please give it to me.*

C2-b use of subject or object form to introduce subordinate clauses

Certain conventions are associated with the choice of pronoun to introduce an adjective (adjectival) clause and, in some instances, a noun (nominal) clause.

C2-b1 inside the adjective clause

To make a sentence into an adjective clause, we cannot simply put the introducing word—known as a *relative pronoun*—in front of the sentence. Instead, we have to replace some word in the sentence with *that* or another appropriate word.

> *that*
> The toys can be put away now. She's tired of ~~the toys~~.
>
> The toys <u>that she's tired of</u> can be put away now.

When an adjective clause is not essential for identifying the entity being talked about, it is introduced by *which* for something that is inanimate—a thing or idea, for example.

> *which*
> Those baby toys can be put away for now. She's tired of ~~those baby toys~~.
>
> Those baby toys, *which* she's tired of, can be put away for now.

The relative pronouns *who* and *whom* can be used to introduce either an essential clause (no comma before it) or a nonessential clause (comma before it). Again, the relative pronoun can be thought of as replacing some element in an underlying sentence.

Review for Test?   Y   N

Phase of writing process
in which to teach:

Review for Test?   Y   N

Phase of writing process
in which to teach:

Grammatical Considerations in Choosing the Right Words

who

Don't throw the ball to any player. ~~The player~~ is not paying attention.

Don't throw the ball to any player *who* is not paying attention.

who

Don't throw the ball to Hank. ~~He~~ isn't paying attention.

Don't throw the ball to Hank, *who* isn't paying attention.

whom

That's the belly dancer. Hector hired ~~the belly dancer~~ for the party.

That's the belly dancer *whom* Hector hired for the party.   OR

That's the belly dancer, *whom* Hector hired for the party.

In the next-to-last sentence, *whom* sounds overly formal; it could simply be eliminated.

C2-b2 inside the noun clause

Some noun clauses are introduced by *who* or *whom*. The conventional choice depends on how the noun was originally functioning in the underlying sentence.

who

I'd like to know SOMETHING. ~~SOMEONE~~ wants to go.

I'd like to know *who wants to go.*

Who is the subject of *wants*. However, in the following sentence, the replaced word is not a subject, so the object form *whom* is called for:

whom

I'd like to know SOMETHING. You've chosen ~~SOMEONE~~.

I'd like to know *whom you've chosen.*

In noun clauses, the pronoun forms *whoever* and *whomever* work like *who* and *whom*:

Give those records to *whoever wants them.* (*Whoever* is the subject of *wants*.)

I'll give them to _whomever_ you have chosen. (_Whomever_ is the object of _chosen_.)

In casual speech and informal writing, we more commonly see the "incorrect" _who_ in sentences such as _I'd like to know who you've chosen_ and _I'll give it to whoever you have chosen_. However, standardized tests call for the use of _whom_.

C2-c agreement in number with noun or pronoun referred to

Here are simple examples of a pronoun not agreeing in number with the noun it refers to:

> The _bikers_ who arrived at the restaurant just as we did parked <u>his</u> bike in a neat row.

> Some example sentences were written to sound like teachers talking to their students, since this supposed _"error"_ has become so common in the speech of educated people that <u>they</u> sound perfectly acceptable to most of us.

In the first example, the word _his_ is singular, but it refers to a plural noun, _bikers_. Therefore, the pronoun does not agree in number with its _antecedent_, the noun it refers to (_ante_ = before). In the second example, _they_ is plural and does not agree with its singular antecedent, _error_.

The preceding examples are simple mistakes, likely to be noticed and corrected in proofreading. However, a less obvious example often occurs when a writer is trying to generalize:

> A _child_ trying to learn something new should have <u>their</u> new kinds of errors honored.

Since _their_ refers to _a child_, this is another example of faulty pronoun-noun agreement: The pronoun does not agree in number with the noun. Such examples are most easily repaired by making the original noun plural:

> _Children_ trying to learn something new should have <u>their</u> new kinds of errors honored.

C2-d pronoun-pronoun agreement

Less obvious agreement issues arise when the subject is an indefinite pronoun that is singular in form but plural in meaning. In the following

Grammatical Considerations in Choosing the Right Words

examples, the later pronoun does not agree with the grammatical number of the subject pronoun:

> *Everybody* should get out <u>their</u> pencils now.

> *Anybody* who wants to can take <u>their</u> project home today.

> *No one* else in the class could write <u>their</u> words as neatly as you do.

In each case, the subject is an indefinite pronoun that is singular in form even though it is plural in meaning: *everybody, anybody, no one*. The example sentences were written to sound like teachers talking to their students, since such supposed "errors" have become so common in the speech of educated people that they sound perfectly acceptable to most of us. However, conservative usage calls for us to avoid using *their* to refer to these singular pronoun forms. If you find it difficult to think of alternative phrasing, you aren't alone.

This particular agreement issue became prominent when the use of the masculine pronouns to refer to everyone, male or female, was challenged. We used to say and write, "Everyone should get out his pencil now," when we meant the entire class, boys and girls, men and women. With increased awareness that such statements seem to exclude females, it became popular to write "Everyone should get out his or her pencil now." But, you may say, this seems unnecessarily awkward. Yes, precisely. That's how the sentences like "Everyone should get out their pencils now" became so common, with the plural pronoun *their* used to refer to a singular indefinite pronoun form.

The conservative prohibition against "Everyone should get out their pencils" is an example of the kind of rule that is sometimes applied by editors at publishing houses but less often honored by writers themselves. However, it is a rule that's often tested by standardized test makers who want to separate those who know conservative usage from those who don't.

C2-e unspecified *they* and *you*

In casual speech and writing, we often use *they* or *you* to refer to unspecified people or to people in general, without meaning anyone in particular:

> <u>They</u> claim they're raising gas prices so <u>you</u>'ll conserve fuel.

Often such statements are made without any context to clarify who "they" is. Is it the gas companies? Some or all of them? The government? What agency or which individuals within the government? It's considered a lapse in logic to use *they* without a specific referent. In the example sentence, *you* is also nonspecific. It seems to refer to people in general. In more formal writing, it's advisable to avoid using *they* or *you* to refer to unspecified persons or groups.

Review for Test? **Y   N**

Phase of writing process in which to teach:

C2-f unclear pronoun reference generally

Sometimes it is genuinely difficult to be sure what noun a pronoun is referring to: The pronoun may be far away from the noun, with other nouns intervening, or the noun may be implied but not stated. The use of the word *them* in the following sentence is perhaps less than crystal clear:

> I also ask students to write one sentence about a read-aloud or any reading. They can write them in their notebooks or on tiny strips of paper that can be given to me as they exit the classroom.

While the meaning is probably clear, the word *them* does not refer to any plural noun in the preceding sentence. An easy way to solve this matter is to replace the pronoun with the noun intended:

> I also ask students to write one sentence about a read-aloud or any reading. They can write these sentences in their notebooks. . . .

In the following example, the noun referred to occurred two sentences before the sentence where the pronoun *they* is used:

> Of course, as the need arises, discussions should be held around the meaning of each of the coordinating conjunctions. Later, they can go back and search more.

In the larger context, it is probably clear that *they* refers to students, not to coordinating conjunctions. Nevertheless, a reader might initially predict that the sentence beginning "Later, they" will be about coordinating conjunctions, since that's the noun that comes right before *they*. It's best to simply change *they* to *students*:

> Of course, as the need arises, discussions should be held around the meaning of each of the coordinating conjunctions. Later, students can go back and search more.

C2-g vague reference with *it, this, that, which*

Grammar handbooks warn against using *it* to refer to something other than a specific noun—perhaps to a concept or idea that has just been specified.

> He couldn't seem to follow the dance steps. It wasn't a matter of not trying; his legs just got tangled up.

> Maria had just found out that she aced her math class. It made her ecstatic!

Most of the time, such uses of *it* are not genuinely confusing. In fact, even the writers of grammar handbooks will typically use *it* and the other pronouns listed to refer to a whole concept or sentence rather than to a specific noun. This is another conservative "rule" that is sometimes tested but seldom followed by published writers. (The immediately preceding sentence is another example of the supposed vague use of a pronoun: *This* refers to the whole sentence before it, not to any single noun.)

Writers need to "correct" the use of *it*, *this*, *that*, and *which* only when a reader will genuinely find the sentence confusing, but they also need to be alert to the possibility of finding such items on standardized tests.

C3 nouns: use of the apostrophe in possessives

Review for Test?   **Y   N**

Phase of writing process in which to teach:

Many writers seem confused about the use of the apostrophe with nouns. The apostrophe is used with a noun only to show possession (loosely construed), ownership, origin, or duration. In the following examples each possessive noun modifies a noun that immediately follows it:

Kim is riding <u>Chet's</u> → motorbike.

<u>Samantha's</u> → notebook is on the counter.

The <u>box's</u> → size isn't quite right.

The <u>fox's</u> → tail is beautiful.

I used to buy <u>Nestle's</u> → chocolate bars. (origin)

Can't you wait even one <u>hour's</u> → time? (duration)

Do I have <u>everyone's</u> → paper? (An indefinite pronoun is made possessive in the same way as a singular noun.)

Speakers of a standard variety of English will automatically add the possessive /s/, /z/, or /əz/ sound in their speech, and usually the *-s* in their writing. The only thing writers need to add, then, is the apostrophe. It goes before the *-s* when the noun is singular, as in the preceding examples. Here are some examples with plural nouns:

That's the <u>twins'</u> two-seater. (It belongs to both twins jointly.)

The <u>foxes'</u> tails are beautiful.

The <u>children's</u> playhouse can go by the picnic table. (The noun is first made plural, and then the 's is added for possessive.)

With plural possessives, the apostrophe goes after the *-s*, except when the plural is irregular. The word *child*, for example, has an irregular plural that does not end in *-s*: *children*. In such cases, add an apostrophe plus *-s* to make the plural possessive: *the children's playhouse.*

The following examples illustrate some other situations with possessives:

John and Chris's house is yellow and white. (When showing joint ownership, only the last noun has *'s*.)

Travis's and Barb's blue jeans are cut very differently. (With separate ownership, make each noun possessive.)

My daughter-in-law's best asset is her patience. (The phrase functions as a unit.)

The masters of ceremonies' voices couldn't be heard above the blaring trumpets. (There are two masters of ceremonies.)

Ordinarily you would not add an apostrophe to a noun that stands by itself, with no immediately following noun:

Harry visited the twins yesterday. [There is no following noun for *twins* to modify, no possessive relationship involved.]

An exception to "don't add an apostrophe to a noun that stands by itself" is a sentence like *the car I'm driving is my friend's.* In the uninverted version, *I'm driving my friend's car,* it is clear that *friend's* is a possessive.

Similarly, a verb form that ends in *-s* or *-es* is not a noun and cannot be made possessive:

Maggie runs the marathon every year.

Gunther washes his car every week.

C4 possessive personal pronouns versus contractions

While nouns take an apostrophe for the possessive, as do pronouns like *everyone's* and *nobody's,* the personal pronouns *my/mine, your/yours, his, her/hers, its, our/ours,* and *their/theirs* are already possessive forms and do not take an apostrophe:

This is his sandbox.

That swing set is theirs.

Let's put yours over here.

The pronoun *its* causes special confusion, because the contraction *it's* takes an apostrophe, as all contractions do:

The terrier lifted <u>its</u> leg by the fire hydrant. (Possessive pronoun.)

<u>It's</u> almost certain what that dog has in mind. (Contraction, short for <u>it is.</u>)

The words *whose* and *who's* contrast similarly. *Whose*, without an apostrophe, is a possessive pronoun in form, although most often it works like an adjective: <u>*Whose book is that?*</u> In contrast, *who's* is a contraction of *who is*. Following is a list of some common contractions.

I am = *I'm*	does not = *doesn't*
he is, he has = *he's*	did not = *didn't*
she is, she has = *she's*	cannot = *can't*
it is, it has = *it's*	could not = *couldn't*
who is, who has = *who's*	should not = *shouldn't*
they are = *they're*	will not = *won't*
you are = *you're*	would not = *wouldn't*
I will = *I'll*	I would, I had = *I'd*
he will = *he'll*	he would, he had = *he'd*
she will = *she'll*	she would, she had = *she'd*
it will = *it'll*	they would, they had = *they'd*
they will = *they'll*	you would, you had = *you'd*
you will = *you'll*	could have = *could've*
are not = *aren't*	might have = *might've*
was not = *wasn't*	should have = *should've*
were not = *weren't*	will have = *would've*
do not = *don't*	let us = *let's*

Contractions are common in speech and informal writing and are sometimes acceptable in more formal writing as well.

Sometimes we see the expressions *could of, would of, should of,* and so forth in students' papers. These forms derive from what the writers have heard in speech. What they are actually hearing, without realizing it, is the contraction of *have* to, just a vowel sound plus /v/: that is, *have* becomes /əv/. The correct written forms are *could've, would've,* and *should've.*

C5 adjective and adverb forms and uses

Two issues regarding adjectives and adverbs are worth mentioning: using conventional comparative and superlative forms, and distinguishing between commonly confused adjectives and adverbs.

Review for Test?   **Y**   **N**

Phase of writing process in which to teach:

| Review for Test? | Y | N |
| Phase of writing process in which to teach: | | |

C5-a comparative and superlative forms

A regular adjective can be compared and made superlative:

slow/slower/slowest
happy/happier/happiest
friendly/friendlier/friendliest
good/better/best (irregular, but the comparative and superlative forms
   still have -er and -est)
reasonable/more reasonable/most reasonable
probable/more probable/most probable
anxious/more anxious/most anxious

In other words, an adjective has not only a base form, but *comparative* and *superlative* forms.

All one-syllable adjectives and some two-syllable adjectives take *-er* for the comparative and *-est* for the superlative, if they are regular adjectives. All three-syllable adjectives and some other two-syllable adjectives take *more* and *most* in front of them to form the comparative and superlative, respectively. When in doubt as to which rule applies to a two-syllable word, use the dictionary.

Avoid double comparatives and superlatives like *more better* and *most fastest*, as well as nonstandard forms like *gooder*.

Sometimes an adverb takes a comparative and superlative, as in these examples: *Drive <u>slower</u> than Tim; drive the very <u>slowest</u> you can.* The same rules for comparative and superlative forms apply.

| Review for Test? | Y | N |
| Phase of writing process in which to teach: | | |

C5-b adjective or adverb form

An adjective modifies a noun; an adverb modifies a verb. Still, it is not always easy to tell which of two words is appropriate in certain instances. *Bad* and *good* are adjective forms; *badly* and *well* are adverbs. In the following sentences, notice how meaning determines the grammatical form needed:

Brad feels <u>bad</u>. (Brad is sick. The adjective *bad* describes the subject, *Brad*.)

Louise, on the other hand, feels <u>good</u>. (Louise is healthy, perhaps even energetic.)

The dog smells <u>bad</u>. (The dog stinks.)

The dog smells <u>badly</u>. (His sense of smell is almost gone; he is not good at smelling.)

The dog smells <u>well</u>. (He is good at smelling things. Maybe he's a bloodhound?)

Notice, though, that when *well* means healthy, it is an adjective: *I feel well*. Misplaced and dangling modifiers are discussed in Section A6.

C6 homophones commonly confused

Perhaps the confusions that educated readers notice most are the incorrect spellings of basic homophones (*homo* = same, *phone* = sound), which sound alike but are spelled differently according to their meaning and/or grammatical use.

C6-a *two, to,* and *too*

Two is the number word that equals one plus one. *Too* has two basic uses: It is used for emphasis, as in *that's too bad*, or to mean "also," as in *I'd like to go too*. All other uses require *to*.

C6-b *your* versus *you're*

Your is the possessive pronoun: *Lift your seat cushion*. In contrast, *you're* means "you are": *You're coming with us, aren't you?*

C6-c *there, their,* and *they're*

The word *there* designates place or is used as an expletive to begin a sentence:

Look at the giraffe over there!

There must be some bear cubs inside the den.

The word *their* is the possessive pronoun: *They all received their diplomas*. In contrast, *they're* means "they are": *They're all ready to go*.

C6-d *its* versus *it's*

As noted before, *its* is the possessive pronoun: *That beaver rebuilds its dam every day*. The word *it's* means "it is": *It's funny how the beaver knows its dam has been compromised*. The contraction *it's*, like the

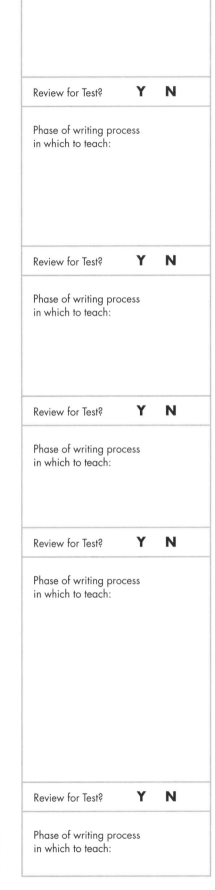

Review for Test?   **Y   N**

Phase of writing process
in which to teach:

Review for Test?   **Y   N**

Phase of writing process
in which to teach:

Review for Test?   **Y   N**

Phase of writing process
in which to teach:

Review for Test?   **Y   N**

Phase of writing process
in which to teach:

Review for Test?   **Y   N**

Phase of writing process
in which to teach:

expletive phrases *it is* and *there are*, can be used at the beginning of a sentence without referring to a specific noun:

> <u>There are</u> many good reasons to leave.
>
> <u>It is</u> a wonder we're all safe.
>
> <u>It's</u> raining ferociously now.

C6-e *whose* versus *who's*

The possessive pronoun form *whose* often works like an adjective, as in *I don't know anyone <u>whose</u> coat that could be*. On the other hand, *who's* means "who is": *Anyone <u>who's</u> still in there at dusk will be stuck there overnight*.

C6-f *accept* versus *except*

Accept basically means "to receive" or "to take": *I <u>accept</u> your offer; I can't <u>accept</u> those test results as valid*. The word *except* has to do with exclusion or leaving out: *Everyone <u>except</u> Paul has brought a permission slip*.

C6-g *affect* versus *effect*

Affect means to have some influence on. It is almost always used as a verb, as in *your speed will <u>affect</u> your test score*. In contrast, *effect* is almost always a noun specifying the result of something: *I'd like to avoid those adverse <u>effects</u>*. (*Affect* can also be used as a noun and *effect* as a verb: *His <u>affect</u> is flat* [no expression on his face]; *exercise alone can <u>effect</u>* [bring about] *weight loss*.) Anyone experiencing basic confusion between *affect* and *effect* is advised to master the most common uses first.)

C6-h *than* versus *then*

Than is used in comparisons: *I am taller <u>than</u> you are*. In contrast, *then* is used to refer to time: *<u>Then</u> I saw what you meant*.

Grammatical Considerations in Choosing the Right Words

C6-i *weather versus whether*

Weather has to do with atmospheric conditions: sunshine, rain, and such. *Whether* means "if."

There are a number of other word pairs that are commonly confused, or pairs for which formal conservative usage requires a choice other than that commonly made. In preparation for a standardized test like the ACT or SAT, reviewing such word pairs is recommended. Some of the practice books for these tests include helpful lists of various word pairs.

C7 eliminating redundancy and wordiness

Redundancy means unnecessary repetition, in this case saying essentially the same thing in more than one way:

Redundant: <u>Today</u> we the people have to stick together <u>in these uncertain times</u>.

Repaired: <u>In these uncertain times</u>, we the people have to stick together.

Redundant: <u>In a few minutes</u> the orchestra should begin <u>soon</u>.

Repaired: <u>In a few minutes</u> the orchestra should begin.
OR   The orchestra should begin <u>soon</u>.

Wordiness is not always so easy to spot, as I know all too well. The following examples are from my first-draft writing:

Wordy: Mostly, of course, it's helpful for teachers whose students are all going to have to take that specific test.

Repaired: Mostly, of course, it's helpful for teachers whose students all have to take that specific test.

Wordy: Typically a small number of students use participial phrases without direct help.

Repaired: Few students use participial phrases without direct help.

Often an unnecessarily wordy construction includes a verb expression like *are going to have to* or a noun with a modifying prepositional phrase like *a small number of students*. These could be simplified to *will have to* and *few students*.

Questions requiring test takers to spot redundancy and especially wordiness abound on the ACT test.

Review for Test?	Y	N

Phase of writing process in which to teach:

Review for Test?	Y	N

Phase of writing process in which to teach:

D | More on Style, Rhetoric, and Conventions

Addressing voice, word choice, sentence fluency, conventions

Writing well involves much more than avoiding errors. In addition to creating compelling, appropriately organized content, good writing involves using precise words, effective modifying constructions, sentence variety, and other rhetorical or stylistic devices. This section discusses choosing between informal and formal variants, emphasizing the most important part of the sentence, choosing between and among punctuation options (with an aside on commas), and ignoring "rules that do not rule" (Schuster, 2003).

<table>
<tr><td>Review for Test?</td><td>Y</td><td>N</td></tr>
</table>

Phase of writing process in which to teach:

D1 | dialects, english-language-learning markers, and informal and formal variants

Certain language choices are more characteristic of identifiable regional, social, or ethnic dialects than others. Technically there is no such thing as a "nonstandard" dialect, because every dialect is standard for the speakers who use it. Students whose native language is not English—often referred to as "English language learners" or "ELL" students—typically use certain features that are not considered "standard." Interestingly, these grammatical markers in their English speech and writing are often very similar, despite very different first-language backgrounds, and often overlap with those in American dialects that are not mainstream, not the language of the marketplace. Mainstream varieties of American English are often called "standard," though there is nothing standard about them, linguistically speaking: They are simply the dialects of those who hold power in government and business. There is greater uniformity in edited American English, so it is a written standard of sorts.

There is no easy answer to the question of how we should refer to the grammatical features of identifiable dialects or to the "interlanguage" grammatical features often used by those learning English as an additional language. Talking about switching from "nonstandard" to "standard" features often generates resistance from students who know full well that the language of their home or peer group is standard for them. Similarly, if we talk about switching from a "dialect" to a more formal version of English, hackles may be raised among students who think their dialect is perfectly adequate and do not want to learn any other language standard, thank you.

In addition, writers who want to use the features of a specific language community to convey a sense of character need to know the features of that particular dialect. It has been said that Mark Twain represented seven different dialects in *Huckleberry Finn* (1895/2001). Other writers have successfully represented other dialects: Claude Brown, for example, even represented sociolinguistic variation within African American English in his novel *Manchild in the Promised Land* (1965).

Linguist Rebecca Wheeler examined writings from many African American students in grades K–16 and identified nine features that occur most frequently. Some of these features are found more generally in Southern speech; some appear in language untouched by education, regardless of the region; and many are found in the speech and writing of English language learners. If your aim as a teacher is to get students to replace these or other informal speech/writing features with the variants used more widely, it is wise to focus on this shift within the context of editing. Marking up their writing with "corrections" will make them afraid to write and inclined to write less and less.

In their book *Code-Switching: Teaching Standard English in Urban Classrooms* (2006) Wheeler and Swords talk about *code-switching* from informal to formal variants and teach it as part of the writing process. Through *contrastive analysis*, they compare and contrast informal with formal variants and lead writers to edit their work to reflect the formal variants in most kinds of public writing. They include nine informal versus formal features on a student editing checklist they call a "Code-Switching Shopping List" (see Figure D–1). Appendix A of their book presents diagrams teachers can use to contrast informal and formal variants of the nine features; their Appendix B lists books (mostly picture books) that include different informal features—books that teachers can share so students can see the informal variants in published literature. Of course, we teachers need to determine which informal variants occur most often in our own students' writing, not simply adopt Wheeler and Swords' list.

D2 foregrounding

The placement of information in a sentence has various effects on the sentence's readability and on the likelihood that readers will remember what they have read. For example, a sentence with a long interrupter between the subject and verb is typically harder to read than a sentence with the free modifiers coming before or after the main subject-verb unit (see the treatment of modifiers in Section A). A *periodic* sentence leads up to

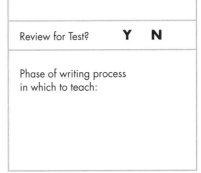

Review for Test?   **Y   N**

Phase of writing process in which to teach:

Code-Switching Shopping List

Name: _____

Do any of the top 10 or so informal English patterns appear in your paper? If so, put a check in the corresponding box and then code-switch to formal English! Add a smiley face, 😊, to show when you use formal patterns in your writing. "Flip the Switch!"

Informal v. Formal English Patterns	Paper 1	Paper 2	Paper 3	Paper 4
1. Subject-verb agreement She walk_ v. She walks				
2. Showing past time (1) I finish_ v. I finished				
3. Showing past time (2) She seen the dog v. She saw/had seen...				
4. be understood He __ cool with me v. He is cool with me				
5. Making negatives She won't never v. She won't ever				
6. be/have + action work He was name_ Tarik v. He was named Tarik A boy name_ Tarik v. A boy named Tarik				
7. Plurality: "Showing more than one" Three cat_ v. Three cats				
8. Possessive (singular) The dog_ tail v. the dog's tail				
9. a v. an An rapper v. a rapper A elephant v. an elephant				
10. Other pattern _____				

FIGURE D–1. Code-switching exercise (By Rebecca S. Wheeler and the Huntington Middle School Writing Project. From Wheeler and Swords, 2006, Appendix A. Used with permission.)

More on Style, Rhetoric, and Conventions

the main subject-verb unit, while a *cumulative* sentence accumulates details after it.

> *Periodic*: Only when the students had studied the contributions of African Americans to science and history, only when they had been allowed to discuss frankly their sense of not being accepted by mainstream society, only when their African American English had been studied for its patterns and its contributions—to rap and soul, preaching and oratory, song and literature—only then were the students willing to learn to code-switch, when appropriate, to a more widely accepted dialect of English.

The main clause, inverted in word order, comes at the end: *only then were the students willing to learn to code-switch, when appropriate, to a more widely accepted dialect of English*. Another term for a periodic sentence is a *left-branching sentence*, because the free modifiers occur to the left of (before) the main clause.

A cumulative sentence begins with the main subject-verb unit:

> *Cumulative*: The girl sat languidly on the dock, her blonde, sun-bleached hair blown back from her face, suntanned legs crossed demurely, eyes squinting toward the middle of the lake where her handsome new neighbor was trying out his first pair of water skis.

This sentence begins with the main clause, *The girl sat languidly on the dock*, and then more and more details accumulate to round out the picture. A cumulative sentence is also known as a *right-branching* sentence.

Often, particularly in informative and persuasive prose, writers will put old, or known, information at or near the beginning of a sentence and new information, or information they want to emphasize, at the end. Putting the new or most important information at the end of a sentence tends to increase the likelihood that readers will remember it. Five sentence patterns help to emphasize important information by putting it nearer the end and/or where the rhythm of the sentence rises for emphasis (Williams, 2005, chapter on emphasis; Kolln, 2003, pp. 51–55).

D2-a sentence inversion with *it*

A sentence that begins with a certain kind of nominal as the subject can be inverted with *it*, so that the important information in the nominal occurs last:

What will happen next is uncertain. ⟶

It is uncertain what will happen next.

Review for Test?   **Y**   **N**

Phase of writing process in which to teach:

That no one has yet won the multimillion-dollar lottery
is amazing. ⟶

It is amazing that no one has yet won the multimillion-dollar lottery.

D2-b **sentence inversion with *there***

A sentence that can be inverted by simply placing *there* at the beginning
normally contains a form of the verb *to be*:

Two bluebirds are perched on my birdfeeder. ⟶

There are two bluebirds perched on my birdfeeder.

Several ticket scalpers were asking outrageous prices for tickets to
the concert. ⟶

There were several ticket scalpers asking outrageous prices for tickets to the concert.

In both of these *there*-inversion sentences, the inversion places greater emphasis on the subject of the sentence.

D2-c **"cleft" sentence patterns**

The *there*-cleft sentence requires the addition of *there*, a form of *to be*, and
that:

Five sentence patterns help to foreground important
information. ⟶

There are five sentence patterns *that* help to foreground important
information.

A sentence like this is called a "cleft" sentence because the underlying sentence has been cleft (divided) in two by the addition of another word, in
this case *that*.

The *it*-cleft sentence is formed in a similar manner:

Daryl, last year's winner, awarded the medal. ⟶

It *was* Daryl, last year's winner, *who* awarded the medal.

The car we bought yesterday got totaled. ⟶

It *was* the car we bought yesterday *that* got totaled.

More on Style, Rhetoric, and Conventions

The added word is *who* in the first sentence but *that* in the second. The *what*-cleft sentence has a similar structure:

They wanted to escape their pursuers.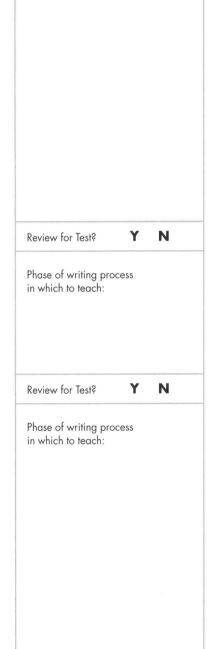

What they wanted *was* to escape their pursuers.

Several deer stood in the road, blocking our way. ⟶

What stood in the road, blocking our way, *was* several deer. (*What blocked our way* is the new subject; being singular, it takes a singular verb.)

The following example is so long that it could hardly start any way other than "It is most important that," or the way the sentence actually starts, "What is [or what's] most important is that":

What is most important is that these individuals' visions become genuinely shared among people throughout all levels of their companies—focusing the energies of thousands and creating a common identity among enormously diverse people. (Peter Senge, *The Fifth Discipline*)

D3 punctuation uses and options

Basic ways of separating and joining sentences were discussed in Section B but with little attention to the less common punctuation marks and their uses: dashes, colons, and semicolons.

D3-a dashes

Teachers often tell students not to use dashes in formal writing, because dashes are so abundantly used in informal writing. Nevertheless, dashes have their functions: to set off parenthetical material; to emphasize something, often at the end of a sentence; and to prepare for a list, a restatement, or an amplification. Type each dash as an em dash, or (the old-fashioned way) as two hyphens, with no space before, after, or between them. Some word processing programs will now convert the hyphens into a dash like we find in published writing.

When a crack develops in our floe and opens at my feet, I jump across it—skillfully, I think—but my jump pushes my side of the floe away, and I wind up leaping full tilt into the water. (Annie Dillard, *Teaching a Stone to Talk*, p. 46)

Review for Test?   Y   N

Phase of writing process in which to teach:

Review for Test?   Y   N

Phase of writing process in which to teach:

We had crossed the mountains that day, and now we were in a stranger place—a hotel in central Washington, a town near Yakima. (Annie Dillard, *Teaching a Stone to Talk*, p. 9)

"Maybe he's rebelling against his dad—the two weren't close." (Robert Ludlum, *The Janson Directive*, p. 180)

Or maybe I should say you were smart—sensing something wasn't right, using the porter to confuse him, putting our friend off balance, buying yourself time to escape. (Robert Ludlum, *The Sigma Protocol*, p. 330)

D3-b colons

A colon is sometimes the more formal equivalent of a dash. Technically, a colon could have been used instead of the dash in the last two examples.

A colon often introduces a list. However, it also functions much more broadly to call attention to something that follows, usually at the end of a sentence. We can think of it as a kind of trumpet, announcing what is to come. Usually what occurs after the colon is more specific than the statement that precedes it: It's as if the writer downshifts or moves in with a zoom lens to specify or be more concrete.

The heirs had expected more: a hint, a clue, something. (Ellen Raskin, *The Westing Game*, p. 74)

When a waiter arrived, a small round man of early middle age, Ben ordered something typically Swiss, heavy and reliable: *Rösti*, roasted potatoes, with *Geschnetzeltes*, or bits of veal in cream sauce, with a *Vierterl*, a quarter-liter carafe of local red wine. (Robert Ludlum, *The Sigma Protocol*, p. 90)

Only one thing mattered: Saturday's big track meet. (Ellin Raskin, *The Westing Game*, p. 124)

But as he approached the darkened city, he began to feel one single emotion: a slowly growing, burning anger. (Robert Ludlum, *The Sigma Protocol*, p. 232)

It was the hubris of the planner that he—he, of all people—had succumbed to: the desk jockey's error of thinking that what worked on paper would mesh with tactical reality. (Robert Ludlum, *The Janson Directive*, p. 69)

This is what actually happened to Tiny: While she was running her lodging house in Seattle, gold was discovered in Alaska. (Willa Cather, *My Antonia*)

The Caliph respected their purity, but his range of experience was far wider, and necessarily so: the master's tools would be needed to

Review for Test?   Y   N

Phase of writing process in which to teach:

More on Style, Rhetoric, and Conventions

dismantle the master's house. (Robert Ludlum, *The Janson Directive*, p. 38)

You know the routine: If the contract is acceptable, please sign both copies and return.

In the last three examples, what follows the colon is a grammatically complete sentence. Opinion is divided about whether to use a capital letter to begin sentences introduced by a colon. (In this book, sentences after a colon do begin with a capital.)

D3-c semicolons

There are two major uses of the semicolon. One is to simultaneously separate and join two closely related independent clauses (simple sentences). We can think of the top part of the semicolon as similar to a period, dividing the clauses, and the bottom part as similar to a comma, joining the clauses; the semicolon does both at the same time. Usually there is either no conjoining word or else a conjunctive adverb (*however, nevertheless, for example*, etc.), though sometimes a coordinating conjunction like *and* occurs after the semicolon. (Some grammar books frown on using a coordinating conjunction after a semicolon, however.)

Everyone was staring; she knew they would notice. (Ellen Raskin, *The Westing Game*, p. 31)

"Why me? I'm a doctor; I took an oath to save lives, not take them." (Ellen Raskin, *The Westing Game*, p. 99)

From ahead, in the foyer, came a female shout, presumably the innkeeper yelling in anger or in fear; suddenly she loomed directly in his path, arms flailing. (Robert Ludlum, *The Sigma Protocol*, p. 116)

We knew we should leave the tavern immediately; nevertheless, there was no way to exit without attracting too much attention. (Semicolon is followed by a conjunctive adverb.)

We sat holding hands, trying to look like innocent lovers; and for a moment, we seemed to have succeeded in our ruse. (Semicolon is followed by coordinating conjunction *and*.)

The other use of the semicolon is to separate items in a series when at least one element in the series has a comma within it:

The judge now knew of four heirs with Westing connections: James Hoo, the inventor; Theo's father; her partner, Sandy McSouthers, who had been fired from the Westing paper mill; and herself. (Ellen Raskin, *The Westing Game*, p. 84)

Review for Test?   **Y   N**

Phase of writing process in which to teach:

When a waiter arrived, a small round man of early middle age, Ben ordered something typically Swiss, heavy and reliable: *Rösti*, roasted potatoes; *Geschnetzeltes*, or bits of veal in cream sauce; and a *Vierterl*, a quarter-liter carafe of local red wine. (Revision of sentence from Robert Ludlum, *The Sigma Protocol*, p. 90)

While a semicolon in published writing is not always the result of one of these rules, the patterns explained and illustrated here are the only ones for which there are rules.

D3-d commas

The primary uses of the comma are to set off nonessential modifiers; to separate items in a series; and, along with a coordinating conjunction like *and* or *but*, to join two independent clauses (simple sentences). These are explained and illustrated in Section A.

Some standardized tests of English—the ACT English test in particular—have a surprising number of questions on the rule-governed uses of a comma, as well as questions designed to see whether test takers know when the use of a comma is *not* sanctioned by some grammar-book rule. By definition, a comma does not occur between an *essential* modifier and what it modifies. In theory, a comma is also not used between the subject and verb of a sentence, between a verb and its object, or between elements of a compound subject or a compound verb or predicate phrase (unless there are three in a series). In practice, published writers do not necessarily follow all of these rules. For example, I frequently put a comma between compound parts of a long predicate, to signal to readers that I want them to pause and process the first part before proceeding to the second. This reader-directed use of the comma is actually quite common in informational and persuasive writing.

D4 rules that don't rule

This section title is borrowed from Edgar Schuster's *Breaking the Rules: Liberating Writers Through Innovative Grammar Instruction* (2003), a book I highly recommend. Schuster in his book and Steven Pinker in *The Language Instinct* (1994) discuss the origins of some of these rules, in addition to offering evidence that renowned writers do not necessarily follow them.

Whether we call them rules that don't rule, myths, or grammatical ghosts (the "living dead" in O'Conner, 2003), there are a number of so-called rules alive in grammar handbooks and teacher staffrooms that promote stilted, unnatural writing rather than the effective prose found in well-written books and articles. The following are some grammar myths

Review for Test?   Y   N

Phase of writing process
in which to teach:

Review for Test?   Y   N

Phase of writing process
in which to teach:

More on Style, Rhetoric, and Conventions

you are encouraged *not* to promote among your students. These are *not* the *descriptive* rules of linguists, who seek simply to describe the language as speakers actually use it. Rather, these are *prescriptive* rules; like a doctor's prescription and advice, they tell us what to do and not to do. Unlike most of the prescriptive rules in this book, though, the following "rules" do not actually rule how published writers write, so I call them *nonrules;* I've selected just a few to discuss. They are presented in no particular order, but are numbered for convenient reference.

D4-a nonrule 1: don't split an infinitive

In English, an infinitive consists of the word *to* plus the basic, or base, form of the verb: *to go, to consider, to explore, to advise,* and so forth. We split infinitives like this frequently: *The mission of the Enterprise is "to boldly go where no one has gone before"; I want to carefully consider my options before deciding; I'd like to actually win a game, for a change.* There is, in fact, no reason for the prohibition against splitting an infinitive, but in the eighteenth century it was popular for grammarians to make up rules for English that were based on the structure of Latin. In Latin, an infinitive can't be split, because it is one word: hence the "rule" to not split an infinitive in English. There is no practical reason to follow this rule, however, and sometimes a sentence sounds really awkward if we do. Would we want to say or write, "I'd actually like to win a game?" Perhaps, but I don't think it means the same as *I'd like to actually win a game.* The authors of *Grammar Alive!* suggest that English teachers should know better than to try to keep students from splitting infinitives, for this is a rule that should have been abandoned two hundred years ago! (Haussamen et al., 2003, p. 72).

D4-b nonrule 2: don't end a sentence with a preposition

This rule, too, was devised to convince writers to make English more like Latin, since ending a sentence with a preposition was impossible in Latin. One reason this rule is inappropriate is that it has been applied to the "particle" associated with a *phrasal verb.* Such verbs include *look up* (locate), *run over* (squash), *tie up* (use), *call off* (cancel), *turn down* (reject, refuse), and literally thousands of other phrasal verbs, according to the *Dictionary of Phrasal Verbs* (COBUILD Staff, 2002). The last word of these phrasal verbs looks like a preposition but isn't functioning that way—nor like an adverb, either. These phrasal verbs can be separated, and the "particle" part may then occur at the end of a sentence:

Ruth called off the meeting.

OR Ruth called the meeting off.

Review for Test? **Y N**

Phase of writing process in which to teach:

Review for Test? **Y N**

Phase of writing process in which to teach:

> For over an hour, Sheila <u>tied up</u> the phone.
>
> OR For over an hour, Sheila <u>tied</u> the phone <u>up</u>.
>
> Jonathan <u>turned down</u> the invitation.
>
> OR Jonathan <u>turned</u> the invitation <u>down</u>.

In short, these words at the end of the second versions may look like prepositions, but they aren't.

However, there is still no good reason, and never was, to prohibit writers from ending sentences with prepositions. Schuster notes that this "rule" has been ridiculed at least since the time of John Milton, who wrote regarding it, "What a fine conformity would it starch us all into!" When a secretary tried to "correct" something written by statesman Winston Churchill in the twentieth century, he is said to have responded in the margin something like, "This is the kind of nonsense up with which I will not put"! Nor should we put up with attempts to keep us from ending sentences with a preposition—or with the particle part of a phrasal verb.

Review for Test?   Y   N

Phase of writing process in which to teach:

D4-c nonrule 3: don't start a sentence with *and* or *but*

And why not start a sentence with *and* or *but*? This is another rule not observed by most good writers, except perhaps in the most formal of writing circumstances. Decades ago, Francis Christensen (1967) examined essays in two "highbrow" publications and found that in their expository essays, almost one out of nine sentences began with *and* or *but* or with another coordinating conjunction (pp. 50–51). Using *but* in this manner is especially common, as it enables the writer to avoid the more formal *nevertheless* or *however*, which may be stylistically too heavy, too stuffy. In this book, I have knowingly started sentences with *and, but, so, or, yet*, and *nor*—all the coordinating conjunctions except *for*, which I personally think subordinates rather than coordinates. Sometimes ending one sentence with a period and starting the next with a coordinating conjunction seems just right to separate yet link two related sentences.

Review for Test?   Y   N

Phase of writing process in which to teach:

D4-d nonrule 4: don't use sentence fragments

Many good writers, including authors of informative and persuasive prose, use an occasional fragment for effect. True, a fragment—grammatically, a piece of a sentence—can be awkward, ineffective, or even misleading (see B5-b), especially when it occurs before the sentence it relates to. However, fragments are often used for emphasis or to capture the natural thought patterns of a character or narrative persona. Fragments abound in the novel *Maniac Magee* (Spinelli, 1990). Here's one example:

The bigger kids came around too, for other reasons. From Moore Street and Arch Street and Chestnut and Green. Heading for the vacant lot to check out the new kid. To test him. To see if everything they'd heard was true. To see how good he really was. And how bad. (p. 54)

The following examples are from Elie Wiesel's *Night* (1960):

"Man questions God and God answers. But we don't understand his answers. We can't understand them. Because they come from the depths of the soul, and they stay there until death." (pp. 2–3)

"Each person will be allowed to take only his own personal belongings. A bag on our backs, some food, a few clothes. Nothing else." (p. 11)

Everywhere rooms lay open. Doors and windows gaped onto the emptiness. Everything was free for anyone, belonging to nobody. It was simply a matter of helping oneself. An open tomb. (p. 15)

The following examples are borrowed from Schuster's *Breaking the Rules* (2003, pp. 111–112):

It [a van] wasn't on the road; it was on the shoulder. My shoulder. (Stephen King, *The New Yorker*)

They are the people who have no homes. No drawer that holds the spoons. No window to look out upon the world. (Anna Quindlen, *Living Out Loud*)

Who can calculate the losses left by Sept. 11? So many wounds to the hearts of families, so many wounds to the souls of New Yorkers, so many wounds to the peace of Americans. (*The New York Times*, 4/11/02, A1).

Kline and Memering (1977) offer categories for the kinds of fragments most often found in published writing; Brosnahan (1976) has done the same for the comma-splice sentence. See Weaver (1996) or Schuster (2003) for summaries.

D4-e nonrule 5: don't use the passive voice

With a grammatically passive sentence, the subject is not the doer of the action; in fact, the doer of the action may not be specified at all. The verb phrase necessarily includes a form of *to be*.

Review for Test?   **Y   N**

Phase of writing process
in which to teach:

The package <u>was</u> carefully <u>wrapped</u> by Miguel.

America's intercontinental railroad <u>was</u> <u>completed</u> by Chinese workers.

The prize <u>was</u> <u>awarded</u> to Ginger.

Ginger <u>was</u> <u>awarded</u> the prize.

The edges of the paper <u>were</u> badly <u>charred</u>.

The murder apparently <u>was</u> <u>committed</u> around 3 A.M.

Some sentences in the passive voice, as it's called, would sound better reworded to place the doer of the action in the subject position. For example, *Miguel wrapped the package carefully* sounds more straightforward and emphatic than the passive version, as does *Chinese workers completed America's intercontinental railroad,* or perhaps *It was Chinese workers who completed America's intercontinental railroad.* But are these versions necessarily better than the passive sentence? It depends, surely, on what the writer wants to emphasize. And what about the other sentences, where the doer of the sentence isn't even specified or needed? The passive has its uses.

D4-f nonrule 6: don't start a sentence with *hopefully*

Why not, you ask? That's a good question, because there is no logical reason to avoid starting a sentence with *hopefully,* any more than there is reason to avoid sentence openers like *finally, eventually, confidentially, seriously,* and other "sentence adverbs" that modify an entire sentence rather than just the verb.

<u>Accordingly</u>, we left a donation on the desk.

<u>Basically</u>, there are only a few important comma rules.

<u>Honestly</u>, I don't know what's wrong.

<u>Supposedly</u> there is only one way through the maze.

<u>Hopefully</u> we will find a simpler alternative.

<u>Hopefully</u>, nobody will hit a home run while we aren't watching.

Steven Pinker (1994) provides an excellent discussion of the absurdity of telling writers not to use *hopefully.*

Review for Test?   Y   N

Phase of writing process in which to teach:

D4-g nonrule 7: don't start a sentence with *there*

It's true that a writer can overuse the expletive *there* at the beginning of a sentence. For example, *There are just a few basic rules covering the use of commas* could be rephrased more succinctly and more strongly as *Just a few basic rules cover the use of commas*. This revision also eliminates an unnecessary *are*. However, as explained earlier in this section, *there*-inversion sentences are sometimes more effective than their untransformed alternatives. And sometimes the suggested alternative doesn't mean exactly the same as the sentence beginning with *there*. For instance, I seem to recall some grammar handbook suggesting that a writer should change *There were many leaves on the ground* to *Leaves covered the ground*. The latter is a stronger sentence, yes, but it implies a lot more leaves than the sentence beginning with *there*!

An excellent article with examples of grammar book writers breaking their own rules is Joseph Williams' "The Phenomenology of Error" (1981). Lynne Truss violates some of the punctuation rules she articulates in *Eats, Shoots & Leaves: The Zero Tolerance Approach to Punctuation* (2003), undermining her diatribe against punctuation rule breakers. No doubt I, too, have broken some of the rules I've described as legitimate—though perhaps my copy editor can save me from public humiliation! (She found one such problem in the very chapter where I talked about avoiding it!)

As I rail against the rules that don't rule, the grammar myths, the "living dead"—whatever you want to call them—I am nevertheless mindful that certain standardized measures like the ACT and the SAT continue to test students for their knowledge of some of these rules. Still, I urge teachers not to limit their students' writing to what is acceptable according to these standardized tests. Good writing is not necessarily grammar-book writing, nor is good writing limited to what is assessed on tests that require a knowledge of conservative grammar-book rules. We need to know which rules most published writers do follow and which they don't. We need to teach our students the difference between writing well and doing well on multiple-choice tests that require not only good revision and editing skills but also a knowledge of rules that seldom rule.

The Grammar Planner

Developing Your Own Scope and Sequence

The letter-and-number designations below correspond with the sections in the Grammar Planner (Part 2). However, teachers are strongly urged not to teach the Grammar Planner text from beginning to end, but rather to select those items that their students need and will benefit from.

Suggested key (you can of course develop your own):

PD	planning, drafting	REV	review
R	revising	RTO	review for test only
E	editing		

Construction or skill	PD/R/E (writing phase)	Grade(s)	REV (review); RTO (review for test only)	Notes
A **Grammar to Expand and Enrich Writing**				
A1 **Adverbials**				
A1-a Adverbial clauses				
A1-b Movable adverbials				
A2 **Adjectivals that are "bound" modifiers**				
A2-a Adjectival clauses				
A2-b Other postnoun adjectivals that are "bound"				
A3 **Prepositional phrases: Adjectival and adverbial**				
A4 **Adjectival words and phrases that are "free" modifiers**				
A4-a Appositives				
A4-b Out-of-order adjectivals				
A4-c Present participle phrases				
A4-d Absolutes				
A5 **Movable adjectives revisited**				
A6 **Dangling modifiers**				
A7 **Parallelism**				

©2007 by Constance Weaver, from *The Grammar Plan Book* (Heinemann: Portsmouth, NH).

Construction or skill	PD/R/E (writing phase)	Grade(s)	REV (review); RTO (review for test only)	Notes
A8 **Comma uses relating to modifiers and parallelism**				
A8-a Opener				
A8-b Interrupter				
A8-c Closer				
A8-d Series separator				
B **The Sentence: Structure, Organization, Punctuation—and More**				
B1 **Subject and predicate**				
B2 **Nominal in the subject function**				
B2-a Noun				
B2-b Noun phrase				
B2-c Pronoun				
B3 **Verbal**				
B3-a **Verb**				
B3-b **Main verb, auxiliary, and verb phrase**				
B4 **Subject-verb agreement**				
B4-a When two compound subjects are joined				
B4-b When a prepositional phrase or other construction separates the subject and verb				
B4-c When the subject and verb are inverted				
B4-d When the subject is an indefinite pronoun				
B5 **Independent clause**				
B5-a Joining and separating independent clauses (simple sentences)				
B5-b Avoiding run-on or comma-splice sentences and ineffective fragments				
B6 **Modifying functions: Adjectival and adverbial** (see sections A1–A6)				
B6-a Adjectival				
B6-b Adverbial				

Construction or skill	PD/R/E (writing phase)	Grade(s)	REV (review); RTO (review for test only)	Notes
B7	**The predicate expanded**			
B8	**Beyond the simple: Subordinate clauses and the complex sentence**			
C	**Grammatical Considerations in Choosing the Right Words**			
C1	**Verbs: Consistency of tense**			
C2	**Pronoun uses**			
C2-a	Use of subject or object form			
C2-b	Use of subject or object form to introduce subordinate clauses			
C2-c	Agreement in number with noun or pronoun referred to			
C2-d	Pronoun-pronoun agreement			
C2-e	Unspecified *they* and *you*			
C2-f	Unclear pronoun reference generally			
C2-g	Vague reference with *it, this, that, which*			
C3	**Nouns: Use of the apostrophe in possessives**			
C4	**Possessive personal pronouns versus contractions**			
C5	**Adjective and adverb forms and uses**			
C5-a	Comparative and superlative forms			
C5-b	Adjective or adverb form			
C6	**Homophones commonly confused**			
C6-a	*Two, to,* and *too*			
C6-b	*Your* vs. *you're*			
C6-c	*There, their,* and *they're*			
C6-d	*Its* vs. *it's*			
C6-e	*Whose* vs. *who's*			
C6-f	*Accept* vs. *except*			
C6-g	*Affect* vs. *effect*			
C6-h	*Than* vs. *then*			
C6-i	*Weather* vs. *whether*			

Construction or skill	PD/R/E (writing phase)	Grade(s)	REV (review); RTO (review for test only)	Notes
C7 **Eliminating redundancy and wordiness**				
D **More on Style, Rhetoric, and Conventions**				
D1 **Dialects, English-language-learning markers, and informal and formal variants**				
D2 **Foregrounding**				
D2-a Sentence inversion with *it*				
D2-b Sentence inversion with *there*				
D2-c "Cleft" sentence patterns				
D3 **Punctuation uses and options**				
D3-a Dashes				
D3-b Colons				
D3-c Semicolons				
D3-d Commas (see sections A8 and B5)				
D4 **Rules that don't rule**				
D4-a Nonrule 1: Don't split an infinitive				
D4-b Nonrule 2: Don't end a sentence with a preposition				
D4-c Nonrule 3: Don't start a sentence with *and* or *but*				
D4-d Nonrule 4: Don't use sentence fragments				
D4-e Nonrule 5: Don't use the passive voice				
D4-f Nonrule 6: Don't start a sentence with *hopefully*				
D4-g Nonrule 7: Don't start a sentence with *there*				

ACT. (2005). *The* real *ACT prep guide.* Iowa City, IA: ACT, Inc.

Anderson, J. (2005). *Mechanically inclined*: *Building grammar, usage, and style into writer's workshop.* Portland, ME: Stenhouse.

Andrews, R., Torgerson, C., Beverton, S., Freeman, A., Locke, T., Low, G., Robinson, A., & Zhu, D. (2004a). The effect of grammar teaching (sentence combining) in English on 5 to 16 year olds' accuracy and quality in written composition. In *Research Evidence in Education Library.* London: EPPI-Centre, Social Science Research Unit, Institute of Education.

Andrews, R., Torgerson, C., Beverton, S., Locke, T., Low, G., Robinson, A., & Zhu, D. (2004b). The effect of grammar teaching (syntax) in English on 5 to 16 year olds' accuracy and quality in written composition. In *Research Evidence in Education Library.* London: EPPI-Centre, Social Science Research Unit, Institute of Education.

Avi. (1984). *The fighting ground.* New York: HarperCollins.

Barrett, J. (1978). *Cloudy with a chance of meatballs.* Illus. R. Barrett. New York: Macmillan.

Beason, L., & Lester, M. (2006). *A commonsense guide to grammar and usage.* (4th ed.). Boston, MA: Bedford/St. Martin's.

Bouchard, D. (1993). *If you're not from the prairie. . . .* Illus. H. Ripplinger. Vancouver: Raincoat Books.

Brosnahan, I. T. (1976). A few good words for the comma splice. *College English, 38,* 184–188.

Brown, C. (1965). *Manchild in the promised land.* New York: Macmillan.

Carroll, J. A., & Wilson, E. E. (1993). *Acts of teaching: How to teach writing.* Englewood Cliffs, NJ: Teacher Idea Press.

Cather, W. (1926). *My Ántonia.* Illus. W. T. Benda. Boston: Houghton Mifflin.

Cazort, D. (1997). *Under the grammar hammer: The 25 most important grammar mistakes and how to avoid them* (2nd ed.). Los Angeles: Lowell House.

Chomsky, N. (1957). *Syntactic structures.* The Hague: Mouton.

Chomsky, N. (1965). *Aspects of the theory of syntax.* Cambridge, MA: MIT Press.

Christensen, F. (1967). *Notes toward a new rhetoric: Six essays for teachers.* New York: Harper & Row. Included in Christensen & Christensen, 1978.

Christensen, F., & Christensen, B. (1978). *Notes toward a new rhetoric: Nine essays for teachers.* (2nd ed.). New York: Harper & Row. Includes Christensen, 1967.

COBUILD Staff. (2002). *Dictionary of phrasal verbs.* Grand Rapids, MI: Zondervan / HarperCollins.

Collerson, J. (1994). *English grammar: A functional approach.* Newtown NSW, Australia: Primary English Teaching Association.

Combs, W. E. (1976). Further effects of sentence-combining practice on writing ability. *Research in the Teaching of English, 10,* 137–149.

Combs, W. E. (1977). Sentence-combining practice: Do gains in judgments of writing "quality" persist? *Journal of Educational Research, 70,* 318–321.

Connors, R. J., & Lunsford, A. (1988). Frequency of formal errors in current college writing, or Ma and Pa Kettle do research. *College Composition and Communication, 39,* 395–409.

Constable, K. (2003). *The waterless sea*. New York: Scholastic.

Culham, R. (2003). *6 + 1 traits of writing: The complete guide grades 3 and up*. New York: Scholastic.

Dillard, A. (1982). *Teaching a stone to talk: Expeditions and encounters*. New York: Harper & Row.

DiStefano, P., & Killion, J. (1984). Assessing writing skills through a process approach. *English Education, 16*, 203–207.

Ellison, R. (1952). *Invisible man*. New York: New American Library.

Erskine, J. (1946). *Twentieth century English*. A later edition, edited by W. Knickerbocker, is published by Ayer in Salem, NH.

Fairclough, N. (1989). *Language and power*. New York: Longman.

Farrell, E. J. (1971). *Deciding the future: A forecast of responsibilities of secondary teachers of English, 1970–2000 A.D.* (Research Report No. 12). Urbana, IL: National Council of Teachers of English.

Francis, W. N. (1958). *The structure of American English*. New York: Ronald Press.

Fries, C. C. (1952). *The structure of English*. New York: Harcourt, Brace.

Gordon, K. E. *The deluxe transitive vampire: A handbook of grammar for the innocent, the eager, and the doomed*. 1993. New York: Knopf.

Great Source Education Group. (no date). *Punctuation pockets*. Boston: Houghton Mifflin. These are file folders, three for different educational levels. Their covers and inside flaps include punctuation rules.

Hacker, D. (2003). *A writer's reference*. (5th ed.). Boston: Bedford/St. Martin's.

Hairston, M. (1981). Not all errors are created equal: Nonacademic readers in the professions respond to lapses in usage. *College English, 43*, 794–806.

Halliday, M. A. K. (1985). *An introduction to functional grammar*. London: Edward Arnold.

Hartwell, P., & LoPresti, G. (1985). Sentence combining as kid watching. In D. A. Daiker, A. Kerek, & M. Morenberg (Eds.), *Sentence combining: A rhetorical perspective* (pp. 107–126). Carbondale, IL: Southern Illinois Press.

Haussamen, B., with Benjamin, A., Kolln, M., & Wheeler, R. S. (2003). *Grammar alive! A guide for teachers*. Urbana, IL: National Council of Teachers of English.

Hillocks, G., Jr. (1986). *Research on written composition: New directions for teaching*. Urbana, IL: National Council of Teachers of English.

Kantz, M., & Yates, R. (1994). Whose judgments? A survey of faculty responses to common and highly irritating writing errors. [Online]. Available at: ateg.org/conferences/c5/kantz.htm. *Assembly for the teaching of English grammar*. [2006, May 20].

Killgallon, D., & Killgallon, J. (2006). *Grammar for middle school: A sentence-composing approach*. Portsmouth, NH: Heinemann.

Killgallon, D., & Killgallon, J. (Forthcoming). *Grammar for high school: A sentence-composing approach*. Portsmouth, NH: Heinemann.

Kline, C. R., Jr., & Memering, W. D. (1977). Formal fragments: The English minor sentence. *Research in the Teaching of English, 11*, 97–110.

Kolln, M. (2007). *Rhetorical grammar: Grammatical choices, rhetorical effects* (5th ed.). New York: Longman.

Kolln, M., & Funk, R. (2006). *Understanding English grammar*. (7th ed.). New York: Longman.

Lester, M., & Beason, L. (2005). *The McGraw-Hill handbook of English grammar and usage*. New York: McGraw-Hill.

Loban, W. D. (1976). *Language development: Kindergarten through grade twelve*. (Research Report No. 18). Urbana, IL: National Council of Teachers of English.

Ludlum, R. (2002). *The Janson directive*. New York: St. Martin's.

Ludlum, R. (2001). *The sigma protocol*. New York: St. Martin's.

Lunsford, A. A. (2003). *The St. Martin's handbook*. (5th ed.). Boston: Bedford/St. Martin's.

Lunsford, A. A. (2004). *The everyday writer*. Boston: Bedford/St. Martin's.

Lunsford, A. A. (2005). *Easy writer: A pocket guide.* Boston: Bedford/St. Martin's.

Lunsford, A. A. (2005). *The everyday writer online.* [CD-ROM]. Boston: Bedford/St. Martin's.

Lowry, L. (1993). *The giver.* Boston: Houghton Mifflin.

McQuade, F. (1980). Examining a grammar course: The rationale and the result. *English Journal, 69,* 26–30.

Mellon, J. C. (1969). *Transformational sentence-combining* (Research Report No. 10). Urbana, IL: National Council of Teachers of English.

Mikaelsen, B. (2001). *Touching spirit bear.* New York: HarperCollins.

Miller, G. A., & Gildea, P. M. (1991). How children learn words. *Scientific American, 257*(3), 94–99.

Munsch, R. N. (1980). *The paper bag princess.* Illus. M. Martchenko. Toronto: Annick Press.

National Council of Teachers of English. (no date). *Professional communities at work: Grammar.* Urbana, IL: NCTE.

Noden, H. (1999). *Image grammar: Using grammatical structures to teach writing.* Portsmouth, NH: Heinemann–Boynton/Cook.

Noden, H. (Forthcoming). *Image grammar activities book.* Logan, IA: Perfection Learning.

Noguchi, R. R. (1991). *Grammar and the teaching of writing: Limits and possibilities.* Urbana, IL: National Council of Teachers of English.

O'Conner, P. T. (2003). *Woe is I: The grammarphobe's guide to better English in plain English.* (2nd ed.). New York: Riverhead Books.

O'Hare, F. (1973). *Sentence combining: Improving student writing without formal grammar instruction* (Research Report No 15). Urbana, IL: National Council of Teachers of English.

Pierce, T. (1997). *Sandry's book.* New York: Scholastic.

Pinker, S. (1994). *The language instinct: How the mind creates language.* New York: HarperCollins.

Princeton Review. (2005). *Cracking the ACT.* New York: Random House.

Raskin, E. (1978). *The Westing game.* New York: Puffin/Penguin.

Roberts, P. (1956). *Patterns of English.* New York: Harcourt Brace Jovanovich.

Rowling, J. K. (2000). *Harry Potter and the goblet of fire.* New York: Arthur A. Levine Books / Scholastic Press.

Rowling, J. K. (2005). *Harry Potter and the half-blood prince.* Arthur A. Levine Books / Scholastic Press.

Rylant, C. (1982). *When I was young in the mountains.* Illus. Diane Goode. New York: Dutton Children's Books.

Schuster, E. H. (2003). *Breaking the rules: Liberating writers through innovative grammar instruction.* Portsmouth, NH: Heinemann.

Senge, P. (1990). *The fifth discipline: The art and practice of the learning organization.* New York: Doubleday.

Seuss, Dr. [Theodore Geisel], & Geisel, A. S. (1972). *Marvin K. Mooney, will you please go now!* New York: Random House.

Smith, W. L., & Hull, G. A. (1985). Differential effects of sentence combining on college students who use particular structures with high and low frequencies. In D. A. Daiker, A. Kerek, & M. Morenberg (Eds.), *Sentence combining: A rhetorical perspective* (pp. 17–32). Carbondale, IL: Southern Illinois University Press.

Spandel, V. (2005). *Creating writers through 6-trait assessment and instruction.* Boston: Allyn & Bacon.

SparkNotes. (2005). *The new ACT.* New York: Spark Publishing.

Spinelli, J. (1990). *Maniac Magee.* New York: Little, Brown.

Strong, W. (1994). *Sentence combining: A composing book.* (3rd ed.). New York: McGraw-Hill.

Strong, W. (1996). *Writer's toolbox: A sentence-combining workshop.* New York: McGraw-Hill.

Strunk, W., Jr., & White, E. B. (2000). *The elements of style*. (4th ed.). New York: Longman.

Truss, L. (2003). *Eats, shoots and leaves: The zero tolerance approach to punctuation*. New York: Gotham / Penguin.

Twain, M. (1885/2001). *The adventures of Huckleberry Finn*. Berkeley, CA: University of California Press.

Vygotsky, L. S. (1962/1986). *Thought and language*. Trans. A. Kozulin. Cambridge, MA: MIT Press.

Weaver, C. (1979). *Grammar for teachers: Perspectives and definitions*. Urbana, IL: National Council of Teachers of English.

Weaver, C. (1996). *Teaching grammar in context*. Portsmouth, NH: Heinemann-Boynton/Cook.

Weaver, C. (Ed.) (1998). *Lessons to share on teaching grammar in context*. Portsmouth, NH: Heinemann–Boynton/Cook.

Weaver, C. (Forthcoming). *Grammar to enrich and enhance writing*. Portsmouth, NH: Heinemann–Boynton/Cook.

Wheeler, R. S., & Swords, R. (2006). *Code-switching: Teaching standard English in urban classrooms*. Urbana, IL: National Council of Teachers of English.

Wiesel, Elie. (1960/1982). *Night*. New York: Bantam.

Williams, J. M. (1981). The phenomenology of error. *College composition and communication, 32,* 152–168.

Williams, J. M. (1986). Non-linguistic linguistics and the teaching of style. In D. A. McQuade (Ed.), *The territory of language: Linguistics, stylistics, and the teaching of composition* (pp. 174–191). Carbondale, IL: Southern Illinois University Press.

Williams, J. M. (2003). *Style: The basics of clarity and grace*. New York: Longman.

Williams, J. M. (2005). *Style: Ten lessons in clarity and grace*. New York: Longman.

Yeats, W. B. (1924). Leda and the swan. In P. Allt & R. K. Alspach (Eds.), *The variorum edition of the poems of W. B. Yeats*. New York: Macmillan, 1957.

Yevtushenko, Y. (1970). *Selected poems of Yevtushenko*. Trans. R. Milner-Gulland & P. Levi. Baltimore: Penguin.

Yoshida, J. (1985). Writing to learn philosophy. In A. Gere (Ed.), *Roots in the sawdust: Writing to learn across the disciplines*. Urbana, IL: National Council of Teachers of English.